Cowley Publications is a ministry of the brothers of the Society of Saint John the Evangelist, a monastic order in the Episcopal Church. Our mission is to provide books and resources for those seeking spiritual and theological formation. Cowley Publications is committed to developing a new generation of writers and teachers who will encourage people to think and pray in new ways about spirituality, reconciliation, and the future.

Playing with Fire

Preaching Work as Kindling Art

David J. Schlafer

Cowley Publications
Cambridge, Massachusetts

Published in the United States of America by Cowley Publications, a division of the Society of Saint John the Evangelist. No portion of this book may be reproduced, stored in, or introduced into a retrieval system, or transmitted, in any form or by any means—including photocopying—without the prior written permission of Cowley Publications, except in the case of brief quotations embedded in critical articles and reviews.

Library of Congress Cataloging-in-Publication Data
Schlafer, David J., 1944-
  Playing with fire : preaching work as kindling art / David J. Schlafer.
  p. cm.
  Includes bibliographical references.
  ISBN 1-56101-269-6 (pbk. : alk. paper) 1. Preaching. I. Title.
  BV4211.3.S35 2004
  251—dc22
                        2004018691

Unless indicated otherwise, scripture quotations are taken from the New Revised Standard Version of the Bible, © 1989 by the Division of Christian Education of the National Council of the Churches of Christ in the United States of America. Used by permission.

Scripture quotations marked NIV are taken from the Holy Bible, New International Version®, copyright © 1973, 1978, 1984 International Bible Society. Used by permission of Zondervan Publishing House. All rights reserved.

Excerpt from "Little Gidding" in Four Quartets, copyright © 1942 by T. S. Eliot; renewed 1970 by Esme Valerie Eliot. Reprinted with permission of Harcourt, Inc.

"She Left Her Water Jar" by Richmond Webster is used by permission of Richmond Webster.

"Come Out, Come Out, Wherever You Are!" by Joy E. Rogers is used by permission of the Joy E. Rogers.

"Taking Up the Cross in a Time of War" by Matthew Gunter is used by permission of Matthew Gunter. This sermon will appear in Preaching as Pastoral Caring: Sermons that Work XII, edited by Roger Alling and David Schlafer (Harrisburg, PA: Morehouse Publishing, 2005).

"People is People" by Elizabeth Kaeton is used by permission of the Elizabeth Kaeton. This sermon, and the sermons by David Schlafer, appear in Preaching Through Holy Days and Holidays: Sermons that Work XI, edited by Roger Alling and David Schlafer (Harrisburg, PA: Morehouse Publishing, 2003).

Cover design: Gary Ragaglia

This book was printed in the United States of America on acid-free paper.

Cowley Publications
4 Brattle Street
Cambridge, Massachusetts 02138
800-225-1534 o www.cowley.org

My role as a nurturing preacher has been a continuing interplay of Priest, Author, Teacher. Three individuals have been *sine qua nons* in the these vocational dimensions—one in each role

In my priesting—James W. Montgomery,
retired Bishop of Chicago

In my writing—Cynthia Shattuck,
former Managing Director of Cowley Publications

In my homiletics teaching—Jack C. Knight, former Dean of Nashotah House, who has been translated into Life Everlasting

For each of these I have high respect, deep gratitude, and great affection. In token of that, *Playing With Fire* is offered in their honor.

Seeing as we are surrounded by so great a cloud of witnesses, let us run with patience the race that is set before us.

Contents

Acknowledgments

A Chorus of Colleagues have lent voice to this volume:
- Kevin Hackett, Michael Wilt, Ulrike Guthrie, and Cheryl Drivdahl, editors and freelance associates at Cowley Publications.
- Richmond Webster, Joy E. Rogers, Elizabeth M. Kaeton, and Matthew Gunter, preaching professionals who have graciously granted me permission to share their sermons.
- Roger Alling, Director of the Episcopal Preaching Foundation, co-editor and co-conspirator in the healthiest of homiletical subversion tactics.
- Susan Burns, Rector, and the Church of the Redeemer, Bethesda, Maryland, the Community of Faith where I worship and share in the ministry of Word and Table.
- A great host of listening preachers in seminary and continuing education settings, among whom insights appearing in this book have been offered and sharpened.
- Dr. Margaret Tucker, scientist, physician, spiritual director, lay healing minister, to whom I am joyfully bonded in ministry and marriage.

Their sound is gone out into all lands, and their words unto the ends of the earth

1

Introduction

Metaphor and Method

This book is an invitation to the art of preaching by way of metaphor. There are other methods—routes more often traveled. The discipline of homiletics is often undertaken via the following:

- Lists of rules, taking learners through the sermon process step-by-step, directing, "First do this, then do that!"
- Catalogues of virtue, setting forth visions of preaching excellence, counseling, "Aspire to this, approximate that!"
- Anthologies of examples, offering specific illustrations of sermon craft, suggesting, "Look at this, listen to that!"
- Treatises of first principles, laying out theological foundations for Gospel proclamation, enjoining, "Understand it as this, undertake it as that!"

The value in such a list of rules is obvious. The territory to be covered in preparing a sermon is vast and complex. How can inexperienced travelers negotiate their way without a map? Catalogue-of-virtue approaches have much to commend them. Traits of character, qualities of life, disciplines of artistic and spiritual temperament—all are sine qua nons of effective preaching. Yet rules and virtues alone are abstractions. Seeing and hearing what good sermons look and sound like is critical ("Oh! That's what you mean! Now I get it!"). And of what avail are instruction and illustration without a framework of first principles—an outline of what it means to preach, and why? It is hardly without reason that preaching texts, course syllabi, and personal mentoring are undertaken by those four methods, individually or in combination.

And yet.

Lists of rules can go on in such detail that sermon preparation looms as an overwhelming enterprise before it is begun. "I haven't time, skill, or energy for all of that," disheartened would-be preachers sigh, casting about for shortcuts (finding excuses, feeling guilty). Homiletical to-do lists can be framed more simply, of course: "Start early! Read the text! Choose a theme! Find good illustrations! Pray without ceasing!" Yet such injunctions seldom spark imagination. And they convey the impression that shaping a sermon is merely a matter of waiting around for the wind of the Spirit. Whether the list of rules is long or short, by-the-numbers preparation often produces paint-by-number preaching.

Vocational visioning, important though it be, seldom helps a harried preacher come up with an idea or connect the dots, especially when time is short and the clock to Sunday is counting down. Every preacher is an individual. No account by a colleague of how to envision preaching can fill the void between a preacher's empty study and an energy-inhabited pulpit.

Books on preaching that proceed *via anthologica* can be valuable resources. But how does one make use of them? As spiritual nourishment, surely. As seeds sown that may someday produce unexpected fruit, definitely! But as specific content or distinctive strategies infused into one's own sermon? If so, how is not clear. Should I cut and paste pieces of good preaching from her sermon to mine? That's plagiarism (or a patchwork of quotations). Emulate his striking style? Easier said than done! (and even if achieved, the effect is the unreal sound of a preaching clone, not the living sound of a preaching voice).

An understanding of why we preach is critical in how we

preach; but saying why is not the same as knowing how. Erudite explanation does not automatically translate into effective expression—many sound sermons don't sound good.

Perhaps the best approach to preaching, then, is all of the above. But simply to add method upon method makes an already formidable task seem all the more unmanageable. So attempting to honor and integrate the values of these methods, we will strike out on an alternative route, approaching the preaching vocation through a dance of metaphors.

Why?

Think of how you learned to swim, to sing, to ride a bike or drive a car. (Not easy, was it?) In each case, learning meant not only more than but other than reading books, memorizing points, checking illustrations, and passing written examinations. Knowledge of physics does not keep you from falling off a bicycle, or sinking to the bottom of the pond! Such skills take practice. Yet "Practice makes perfect" is probably not a perfect description of how you actually learned to swim or sing, bike or drive. Practice by itself can build bad habits and produce disastrous results: waterlogged lungs, sore throats, skinned knees, and dented fenders.

What one needs for mastering these practices, and what you had if you were lucky, is a teacher, a coach, or a colleague who can name what one is feeling in the process of learning how ("Don't hit the water; it's your friend! Let your body be a feather, floating on the wind!"). Such naming helped you learn—and continue to gain proficiency. Naming by means of metaphor focused, directed, and evoked your energy along the learning pathway. Naming by metaphor led you through stage after stage: getting an initial feel, internalizing the basic moves, employing advanced skills creatively (as patterns first thought about painstakingly and tried awkwardly eventually become ingrained as habit).

Once your skill admitted you to a guild of artists, hobbyists, sports enthusiasts, or working professionals, metaphors provided a common metalanguage for celebrating achievements, comparing notes, and conducting healthy collegial criticism ("To get sunlight dancing on the water like that, I had to caress the canvass with my brush"; "If you want a rhythmic feel in this section of the speech, try punching some of the phrases a bit, and balancing the sentences overall"; "Don't kill the ball—just meet it").

Metaphors foster kinesthetic vision. They serve as centering reference points among colleagues-in-learning because they make sense at conceptual, practical, and visceral levels simultaneously. Metaphors offer words and images for common practices that participants in a process can internalize individually, uniquely, and at different stages in their learning. Well-focused metaphors provide shared meeting places, places of connection, resonance, and professional discussion with others engaged in the practice. Metaphors are critical in sparking productive energy across the gap between theory and practice. Metaphors also foster the seemingly ineffable but absolutely essential synergistic dimension of learning. They help us to assemble, integrate, and incorporate the many elements, subtle and unnamed, distinct but interrelated, that constitute creative artistry. Metaphors are perhaps the best teaching techniques at our disposal, whether we are trying to learn or trying to help others learn. Have you doubts about the significance of metaphor as a vehicle for learning? Check out those doubts with a teacher named Jesus; he resorted to metaphors on all sorts of occasions. Matthew, chapter 13, is a place to start your search.

Two metaphors dance together across the pages of this book: fire and play. Two metaphors, plus a hunch: that texts of the Scriptures, the grounding voices of inspiration for Christian preaching, offer more than just truths to be interpreted and transmitted. What we call the Scriptures are the work of a great company of preachers. The Bible is a treasure lode of imaginative insights regarding how the

5

mystery of preaching might be entertained.

Consider: throughout the history of human experience and across the pages of the Holy Scriptures, fire recurs as a metaphor for describing what happens when the power of a transcendent God touches the fragile world of flesh and blood. This constant comparison can hardly be coincidental. Fire is multisensory and mysterious, life nurturing and life threatening. Fire is as difficult to define conceptually as it is hard to contain physically. Yet the experience of fire is never vague, always vivid. Fire is elusive, in constant change. Fire cannot be pinned down, but it is no abstraction! Perhaps that is why so many biblical authors in so many different settings resort so often to fire when they seek to describe the surging energy of a God who acts in love to shape, cleanse, heal, cast down, and raise up—all in relentless determination to make the whole creation new.

The history of preaching is a story of sacred fire sharing—of passing on a power beyond all human capacity to generate or to contain. How can those called to proclaim the Gospel appropriately tend and transmit this fire? Perhaps by playing with it.

Preaching as play? Preposterous! Preaching is hard work, serious business! Nothing to play around with! Playing with fire is dangerous, particularly if the fire is from God! The misappropriation of divine fire has wreaked horrendous devastation. People have been badly, wrongly burned by preaching. Metaphorically. Literally. But . . . What if—at its heart, and when it's right—preaching is really a headlong plunge into the surging energy through which God calls worlds into being, and refashions worlds afresh, when they have torn themselves apart? What if preaching could be participation in God's own sacred play? How might those in the pew and those in the pulpit experience it that way?

In what follows, we will appropriate fire images from a wide range of biblical texts, using them primarily as gestures toward the power and presence that preachers are called to proclaim. We will employ play images primarily to convey a feel for principles and processes that constitute the discipline of proclamation artistry.

Chapter 1 grounds preaching in the play of the Creator whose first word is *fire*. Chapter 2 pauses to raise second thoughts about whether it is appropriate or possible for mortal wordplayers to share in shaping the sight and sound of sacred fire—let alone to do so playfully. (These first two chapters, therefore, are an initial attempt to honor treatises-of-first-principles approaches to preaching.) Chapter 3 invites us to explore how and where God's fire has broken out at various times and places across the heartscapes of our lives, since preachers are not themselves untouched by what they have been called to transmit. (This will engage concerns highlighted in catalogues-of-virtue preaching methods.) Chapters 4–6 outline an interplay of preaching strategies and preparation stages that reflect appreciation for lists-of-rules approaches, but with more space for openness to the Spirit's continual urgings toward outbreaks of reverent creativity. Chapter 7 addresses an issue of particular urgency: How can we discern the difference between appropriate and misdirected manifestations of preaching fire? Chapter 8 places preaching in the context of Pentecost, asking how those among whom we preach can more fully participate in the process. Chapters 9–10 move back in the direction of virtues and first principles approaches to homiletics, 9 considering how we are transformed by the fire we transmit, and 10 attempting a fragmentary glimpse of New Creation light—the eschatological energy articulate in every play of preaching fire. Occasional sermon samples are offered en route. Welcome to the adventure!

7

1

Let There Be Light!

In the beginning when God created the heavens and the earth, the earth was a formless void and darkness covered the face of the deep, while a wind from God swept over the face of the waters. Then God said, "Let there be light"; and there was light. And God saw that the light was good. (Genesis 1:1–4)

"Come out and play!" What does the sound of that call signal? Maybe you are six years old. Or sixteen—twenty-three—even eighty-seven. What will you do if you heed the call? Make mud pies? Join a slugfest of outrageous puns? Build a snow fort? Play tag (or chess)? Try on old clothes from the attic— then try on a role that fits the clothes, though the clothes don't fit at all? With whom will you play? A gaggle of neighborhood kids? The bridge club? A cell of soul mates? A cybercompanion?

"Let's play!" Do you want to join in? Of course! Who doesn't want to plunge headlong into the energizing fire of happy play? What's to say but, "Here I come!"

Unless you've been burned before. Being played with has negative connotations too. You can be dragged against your will into a game at which you aren't any good. You can be set up for ridicule as the object of somebody's joke. You can be manipulated by people who play games with you. But those are perversions of play, are they not? They are not what play is really about!

"Come out and play!" Even if a bad play experience leaves you feeling guarded or wounded, the yearning to share in what play is meant to be is hard to smother. Safe spaces for play are employed therapeutically to heal the effects of destructive play. Manifestations of spirited play are as multiform as culture, experience, imagination, and taste. What is attractive play for me may be uninteresting to you. Yet the feel of the event serves as a point of contact between us even if you have no interest in playing as I do. Have you ever chuckled while listening to someone describe a fondly remembered time of play? Such self-disclosure makes the speaker vulnerable. And you laugh! But you aren't laughing at the person. You are indulging in a spontaneous celebration of shared satisfaction: "I'd never do that; but I know what you mean. In my own ways of playing, I've been there too."

How do we define play? Suppose we observe a broad spectrum of people caught in the act: children skipping stones across a pond, teams mixing it up in a contact sport, individuals absorbed in games of solitaire, everyone singing and dancing at a folk music festival. What is the connecting thread? What do such different activities have in common? What does it mean to play?

That is not an easy question. We often contrast play with work. We tend to identify play with what we want to do in contrast with what we have to do. Play is sometimes equated with escape, either approved ("Everyone needs time to play!") or disapproved ("Quit your playing and get busy!"). Play is what we do on our own time—when we are off duty ("Class is over for now, children; go play on the playground!").

But the matter is not so simple. Schoolchildren may experience play periods as prison terms (I sometimes did!). On the other hand, schoolwork (or housework, garden work, even office work) can sometimes be a hoot—refreshing, energizing—indistinguishable in tone from any event conventionally designated as play. Deliberate play can become so absorbing that one expends far more energy on it than on work!

Playing with Fire: Preaching Words as Kindling Art

What makes activities playful? A texture of feeling and focus, a quality of experience interwoven through action. Ask people why they like to ride bikes, read books, take hikes, or simply sit in silence, and you get a fairly consistent pattern of responses: "This is play for me because when I undertake it, I feel a sense of freedom, community, adventure, and creativity." Let's linger a little over each of those feelings.

Freedom is not simply an absence of constraint, a stream of random behaviors. Feeling spaced out is not feeling free. Freedom always involves focus—an intentional spark of energy, dependent for combustion on a set of givens. How free would you feel to swoop on a big old tire swing if the links of the chain connecting it to the sturdy tree limb were all but rusted through? What would freedom mean if you couldn't depend on your arms and legs to pump you higher as your mind kept nudging them harder? Freedom always involves an interplay between elements of spontaneity and structure.

Community is an essential element in play as well. Children (and adults) sometimes play by themselves, perhaps because doing otherwise is painful or impractical, but maybe just because they want to. A person curled up in a quiet space with a good book has not made a Cartesian withdrawal. (Even Descartes needed the Evil Demon to help him prove the certitude of his own existence!) No. To read to yourself is to participate in a populated world. What often spells the difference between whether or not you want to keep playing is how comfortable you feel interacting with playmates. We touch the freedom of play when we enter a setting where colleagues contribute without controlling. Community is companionship that welcomes the distinctive individuality of each participant. It is next to impossible for play to take place without some sort of teamwork. Games of solitaire have dummies. Children home alone have TV comrades or imaginary friends. Rare are the individuals who, when all by themselves, don't talk to themselves. I do; don't you?

Adventure always surges through experiences of healthy play.

10

Play is hardly ever aimless; it has an object. Those in play are always en route: trekking, questing, reaching, wrestling, winning (or losing), coming back and celebrating (or commiserating). Some sort of accomplishment must loom on the horizon as a live possibility in order for play to commence. Yet each achievement must yield to further challenge if play is to be sustained. Play isn't any fun if there isn't any point. Play isn't worth the effort if the journey is devoid of obstacles—even a measure of threat. Still, if there is no undergirding sense of security, the adventure of play quickly turns terrifying. In other words, adventure is an interchange of open-ended challenge and satisfactory closure—undertaken in an atmosphere of both risk and safety.

Creativity is probably the single most significant dimension of play. It infuses ordinary materials with extraordinary meaning. Some examples:

- A group of folks square off with a stick of wood, a small sphere, and four flat rocks. Suddenly, a baseball game!
- A six-year-old pulls a big towel from its bar on the bathroom door, drapes it from his shoulders, and sweeps through the house. He's a superhero!
- Three friends join forces stroking horsehair strings stretched taut on wooden rods over strings stretched taut on odd-shaped wooden frames, all the while attending to tiny black splotches spattered over parallel lines on sheets of paper. The result—a violin trio. (They call it an opus, but they play it nonetheless.)

Creativity: worlds of meaning built on and shaped out of raw materials—materials that are necessary, but insufficient, for bringing into being the richer, deeper worlds of game, drama, and music.

You see where this is leading—straight into the once-upon-a-time of the Genesis Creation stories. "The earth was without form, and void, and darkness was upon the face of the deep. And the Spirit of God moved upon the face of the waters. And God said, 'LET THERE

BE LIGHT.' And there was light!" Shapeless stuff shaped into worlds. Awesome worlds ignited by words.

Why do we play? Because we are made by God to be like God. *Imago dei—homo ludens*: the image of God is humanity at play. At the explicit command of our Maker, we make worlds of many-layered meaning, doing so by words.

Mud pies and music, made with words? Not words alone. We also have to get our fingers dirty (or get them trained). But words are involved. Words can, in fact, be decisive actions in themselves. Words perform. Words make things be. Language creates universes of discourse that convene communities that, in freedom, undertake adventures of creative expression.

Creation is the drama of "Let there be! There was light; and it was good!" As creatures of God, we get to play too. God lets us be. We were made to be, we are, co-creators with God. Freedom, community, adventure, and creativity: that's where play starts from, and what it's for.

What God does in the Creation becomes God's modus operandi for dealing with the world. The motif is clear in God's covenants—in the agreements God makes with Adam, Noah, Abraham, and Moses; in the new thing God announces through Isaiah; in what God gives in promise to Sarah and Hannah, does through Ruth and Esther, and comes and does in Jesus Christ (and in new-covenant activities in the life of the church, like baptism and the Eucharist). God is forever taking whatever stuff is lying around and at hand (which, after the Fall, is battered, broken stuff indeed), and making all things new. Freedom, community, adventure, and creativity: the Word of God, without denying the givens, lifts them up, plays the pieces afresh, transforming what is as good as dead into something alive and better.

The fire God ignites by saying, "Let there be light!" is not restricted to the Creation stories. God plays with fire across the sweep of sacred history. What commences in Genesis lights the biblical

12

landscape all the way to the end of Revelation:

- From a flaming sword that bars the first couple's reentry into Eden, to a burning bush that transfixes an Egyptian prince turned Hebrew herdsman
- From a moving pillar that protects refugees at the Sea of Reeds, to an eruption on Mount Horeb that all but scares those poor vagabonds to death
- From descending flames that transform offerings into ashes, to fiery chariots that surround one prophet for safekeeping and transport another up into heaven
- From an unquenchable fire that incinerates chaff, to irrepressible tongues of flame that ignite a Pentecost unlike any other
- From a cooking fire on a lakeshore that sizzles breakfast fish, to the Lamb of light, who sends a radiance across heaven that precludes the need for any other lamp

Throughout the pages of the Holy Scriptures, God is forever playing—playing with fire.

Well, if God can, we can. After all, God said we should. God shares the gift and expects us to use it. What does that mean? The work of the preacher is no indirect, secondhand service. The mighty acts of God all have to do with freedom, community, adventure, and creativity. Preaching has to do with these as well.

Preachers do not proclaim themselves. Strictly speaking, we cannot, even if we want to (though we sometimes seem to give it a try). We couldn't proclaim had we not been ignited by the Word of God's power. Even when we understand our job and try our best, the words we employ only gesture in the direction of divine fire.

Yet preaching the Gospel is not simply delivering laboriously crafted sermons to instruct, explain, exhort, cajole, rebuke, console—to speak, as it were, on God's behalf. Preaching is not just talking about God's play of fire; preaching is participating in, actively entering into the divine energy of freedom, community, adventure, and creativity. Preaching is playing with fire.

Indeed, the Scriptures that speak of God's incessant incendiary action are replete with stories of how those called to speak for God are swept into the center of the energy. The prophet may proclaim, "Thus says the Lord," but what the prophet says is not simply a fax, delivered through a machine. Try telling Ezekiel, as he stands before a valley of dry bones, that his message is just a printout of God's words. In the words of the preacher, the breath of mortal joins with the breath of God. The Word of the Lord resounds through a human larynx—and only then do dry bones stand on the earth alive.

Ezekiel's experience is not unusual. Let your memory run free over the pages of the Scriptures. It will take you no time to generate a long list of preachers plunged into the holy terror and utter joy of playing with fire.

And what is true for those preachers is also evident in the sermon notes they have left behind. Consider how the characters and speakers of the Scriptures make their cases: song singers, storytellers, vision painters, analytical trapeze artists (St. Paul is nothing if not one of these!). Each calls worlds into consciousness, striking fire by means of words. All, in ways uniquely appropriate to their distinctive God-given artistries, create multidimensional spiritual effects out of one-dimensional signals.

With a word, the psalmist evokes an orchestra of jubilant praise. With a word, the author of the Apocalypse creates breathtaking multimedia visions that alternately awe, terrify, and reassure. With a word, the prophet buries listeners under a crushing avalanche of consequences that have been set in motion by arrogant words of the listeners themselves. With a word, the prophet sends a shaft of hope shimmering down into the open cracks of a tomb given up for sealed.

Consider the teaching of Jesus. His words heal—not primarily by sheer command, but by inviting his hearers into unimagined

14

worlds. Worlds where, for instance, the Reign of God is likened to—how's that again?—a grain of wheat, a mustard bush, a stumbled-on treasure, a long-sought pearl, a mixed bag of fish. In case after case, the light of insight comes through playing with fire. If these preachers can do it, so can we. But how?

2

God Is a Consuming Fire

*Since we are receiving a kingdom that cannot be shaken, let us give thanks,
by which we offer to God an acceptable worship with reverence and awe;
for indeed our God is a consuming fire.* (Hebrews 12:28–29)

How can we play with fire? Play and fire may gesture toward what
God does, but how do they apply to what we do? As possible
metaphors for preaching, they may tickle the imagination and spark
spontaneous energy. But so what?

How does the invitation to preaching issued by those
metaphors help us get the job done? How can those metaphors
serve—let alone better serve—the mentoring function undertaken
by other introductions to homiletics we have named? Preachers do
have to go through preparatory steps; they must undertake a process
informed by high ideals, clear examples, and first principles. Addressing this strategic "How do we proceed?" question is the primary
thrust of this book.

The question "How can preachers play with fire?" names another concern as well: Not so much "How do we proceed?" as "How
do we dare?" Who are we, creatures frail and broken, to play with fire
in the practice of preaching? This is no mere rhetorical question; it
goes to the heart of our vocation. As important as sermon procedures
and techniques may be, they pale in significance against the sober-

ing reminder from the author of the Letter to the Hebrews: "Our God is a consuming fire." The prophet Malachi (3:2) brings this observation even closer to home: "Who can stand when he appears?" These preachers prompt second thoughts about undertaking preaching as playing with fire.

Why do so many biblical writers speak of encounters with the Holy One in terms of vivid experiences with fire? Probably, I suspect, because of the incredibly rich connotations of that natural phenomenon. An outbreak of fire almost never goes unnoticed. Attention is invariably drawn to fire. Fire is a multimedia event, engaging all our senses. We can see its color, hear its crackle, feel its heat. Most fires have a distinct smell. Even our taste buds, connected as they are with olfactory receptors, go on the alert in the presence of fire.

Fire comes in many shapes and sizes, from contained, quiet candle flames to uncontainable, thundering firestorms. Fire manifests itself in many forms—yellow campfires, blue gas flames, brilliant white lightning flashes, seething red lava. Fire performs a wide array of functions that impact human life: cooking, illuminating, signaling, gathering creatures together (and warding them off), creating wounds (and cauterizing them). Fire reduces fuel to ashes, refines away impurities. It decimates forests—and in so doing creates conditions necessary for new life.

Fire evokes feelings as complex and contradictory as its functions. Fire can engender comfort and alarm, sheer delight and stark terror. It produces curious interest and complete fascination. Children are constantly poking at fires—children of all ages. We don't seem to be able to leave fire alone. People attempt to control fires, with limited success. There are disciplines for fostering or fighting various fires, precautions for dealing with fire responsibly. But now and again, fire just breaks out and consumes.

It is not surprising that such a multifaceted phenomenon should serve as a symbol for a wide range of human experiences: illu-

17

minating insight, focused energy, sparkling enthusiasm, raging hate, unquenchable love. Regardless of what benefits it may provide or delight it may evoke, fire always comes with warning signals: Danger! Do not touch! Handle with care! This power is awesome, unpredictable, life-threatening (even though, in some sense, your life depends on it). Fire attracts and repels us all at once. What better metaphor—not a term, a concept, or even a force—can we use to say what it is like to encounter the inescapable, uncompromising Living Presence? The author of Hebrews says it well: "It is a fearful thing to fall into the hands of the living God" (10:31).

It is not surprising, therefore, that, for all the uniqueness of face and circumstance, everyone receiving a call from God in the Scriptures responds with spontaneous terror and humility: "I am 'sore afraid'! I cannot speak your word!" To that terror, God often responds, "Fear not!" Yet God never says: "Don't worry! It's only me! This is no big deal!"

That is a curious phrase, "Fear not!" A command—an absurdly impossible one. It is at least as curious a phrase for God to use as the statement "Fire is nothing to be afraid of" would be for us to use. Yet, having appeared and issued the call, God commands the impossible and proceeds to make it happen. God comes in fire, sets us alight, and commissions us to pass the flame on.

But not so fast. It is no quick move from the claim that humans cannot speak for Consuming Fire, to an assurance that they easily can. It is one thing to be released from fear in the presence of the Fire, quite another to presume to speak on the Fire's behalf. And preachers can be presumptuous! How perilously simplistic it is to go from Jeremiah's "Is not [God's] word like a fire?" to "I can set words on fire—so my words are God's words." Tempted to try that gambit, we would do well to drop in on a fellow professional, Elijah, a prophet who experienced God's fire. And didn't.

There he stands on a mountain called Carmel, with an offering

18

to his God. All Israel is arrayed before him, and four hundred prophets of Baal as well. This is a test, a critical experiment. "The God who answers by fire is God!" Elijah thunders. To heighten the effect that he fully anticipates, Elijah directs the offering to be thoroughly doused with rivers of water. He calls upon heaven; the flames descend. Prophecy just doesn't get any better than this!

But, alas, once Elijah brings the false prophets to an untimely end at the point of his sword, their patron Jezebel (understandably displeased) dispatches to Elijah a promise of analogous treatment. Elijah cuts and runs, flees in terror to the mountain of God, the very place where, once upon a time, the Word of the Lord descended in fire and smoke. Fire comes again, all right. But the Scriptures tell us that "the Lord was not in the fire." God showed up, rather, in "the sound of sheer silence" (1 Kings 19:12).

Somewhere in that story is a moral for fire-breathing preachers. Not all their fire necessarily flows from God. Another preacher (James 3:6,8) from a different time and place (but just as outspoken as Elijah) puts the matter in graphic terms: "The tongue is a fire. . . . [It] sets on fire the cycle of nature, and is itself set on fire by hell." "No one can tame the tongue," he insists. "It is a restless evil, full of deadly poison." By the tongue, we bless God, and by the same tongue, we curse God's children. "What is wrong with this picture?" he asks!

It is a picture we have had to face over and over, in city after city. Torrents of deadly fire unleashed—kindled, in no small measure, by incendiary words shot from self-righteous tongues. The pictures give fresh credibility to the words of James, who is sometimes dismissed as a moralistic tongue minder.

How, indeed, do preachers undertake the kindling art? Clearly, God's Word is like a fire. And, as Jeremiah observes, that fire sometimes burns uncontained within our bones. But despite the apparent simplicity of those claims, things quickly become confusing. God's fire sometimes seems withering, painful, and scorching, with no apparent redeeming mercy in view. And so, it would seem to follow, a preacher's fire will sometimes need to bring something less welcome than "comfort, light, and fire of love," as the familiar hymn puts it (*Veni Creator Spiritus*, in *The Hymnal*, #503/504).

The fire of God's judgment cannot be equated with or used to justify the fires of inquisition—verbal, let alone physical. How, then, is a preacher to know when the fire he or she feels called to bring is the proper sort of heat and light? Making that determination isn't a simple matter of monitoring the temperature and measuring the candlepower (not to mention decibels!) of one's language. A fire that is kindled oh, so carefully cannot be certified as God's simply by reference to good intentions, pure motives, or the overall quality of spiritual life.

What, for a preacher, spells the difference between sermons that light up the world like the Eiffel Tower at the celebration of the new millennium, brilliant in pyrotechnic splendor, and sermons that bring tragically misguided messages of judgment like those the hijackers imposed on the Twin Towers on September 11? How nice it would be if we could respond, "Celebration sermons are just fine; but no hint of condemnation must ever be uttered." It certainly doesn't work that simply for the Scriptures' prophets. Not all sermonic celebrations pass muster. Consider the blessings of empire and promises of prosperity that pour from the mouths of those whom God's real prophets attack as insidious spin-artists, babbling on and on about "the temple of the Lord"! Consider the withering criticisms that are delivered by God's spokespersons and turn out to be the death of them.

No. There are no full and flawless checklists for identifying authentic fire from God. And no guarantees, either before the act or after the event, that we will be able unerringly to spot false (potentially disastrous) look-alike flames—in the preaching of others or in our own. But there may be some clues, some indicators we can come to trust. Let us return to the observation from the author of Hebrews:

Since we are receiving a kingdom that cannot be shaken, let us give thanks, by which we offer to God an acceptable worship with reverence and awe; for indeed, our God is a consuming fire.

In that statement, the phrase "consuming fire" may initially draw our attention. But other phrases might reach out and catch it as well:

- *"We are receiving a kingdom that cannot be shaken."* What we receive is a gift, and not an elusive, ephemeral one.
- *"Let us give thanks."* Preaching is first and foremost an act of thanksgiving, not an act of threatening, persuading, impressing, or even just speaking.
- *"We offer to God acceptable worship."* The proper way we respond to gift is with gift. Having received a kingdom (whatever that entails), we draw on its resources to make what might be called a very limited contribution in kind. The fire we share is one we pass on, not one we start up; the moves of play that we undertake derive from moves that God first makes.
- *"With reverence and awe."* We respond to God with neither hero worship nor paralyzing dread, but rather an inextinguishable reticent eagerness that comes from a surprising, insistent invitation into the middle of a mystery that is both totally beyond our reach and far too wonderful to miss!

These observations themselves don't move us very far toward what we will take into the pulpit next Sunday! But for the moment, we are deliberately lingering over the "How, indeed?" question—not in its "How do we proceed?" form, but rather in its "How do we dare?" permutation. In other words, to talk about preaching as a holy gift of thanks for a holy gift received is to set a frame of reference for playing with fire. It is a frame of reference that, while not answering the practical questions (or dissolving the healthy spiritual dilemmas), is not entirely devoid of practical import. The longer we dwell with our fellow preacher's admonition to his congregation in the Letter to the

Hebrews, the closer we find ourselves moving deeply into that felt rhythmic interaction of freedom, community, adventure, and creativity that sparks and characterizes the play of creation as well as the interesting juxtaposition of *imago dei* and *homo ludens*.

Sermons that burn listeners, that play with their minds and their feelings, that assault or seduce them (supposedly for their own good) are perversions of preaching as fire and as play. But so are sermons that neglect listeners' deep needs by failing to invite them into serious, even strenuous, but nonetheless joyful re-creation with God. If and when preachers fail in their vocation, God will not. Therein is the warning for preachers, and also the grace. For, indeed, our God is a consuming fire.

3

Burning but
Not Consumed

Moses was keeping the flock of his father-in-law Jethro, the priest of Midian; He led his flock beyond the wilderness, and came to Horeb, the mountain of God. There the angel of the LORD appeared to him in a flame of fire out of a bush; he looked, and the bush was blazing, yet it was not consumed. (Exodus 3:1–2)

God is a consuming fire, says the author of Hebrews. Recounting God's call to Moses, the Exodus storyteller declares that the bush God enkindles to get Moses's attention is not consumed. Set in the canon of the Scriptures approximately midway between these two narratives is a story about a Babylonian execution chamber—a fiery furnace. King Nebuchadnezzar, beside himself with fury, has the furnace stoked with a fire seven times hotter than usual. Overkill, if ever there was such a thing, for the flames incinerate even the executioners. Yet Shadrach, Meshach, and Abednego, the intended victims of imperial ire, emerge from the furnace unscathed—protected by the One who, to the incredulous eyes of His Majesty, has "the appearance of a God" (Daniel 3:25).

God, a consuming fire, does not consume the burning bush, and counters the intended consuming effects of a human fire, pre-

23

serving the three Hebrew children by showing up in a way that can all but be characterized as fighting fire with fire.

What are we to make of such apparently discrepant descriptions? Critical studies of the Scriptures deal with many dimensions of distinction in biblical voices. Those studies are important means of ensuring that those voices have a chance to speak for themselves, instead of becoming mere echoes of our own. Methods of biblical interpretation need to be undertaken with energy as reverent acts of intelligent worship. And yet, as philosopher-theologian Paul Ricoeur notes, effective understanding and proclamation of the Scriptures requires a "second naïveté." As we mature, we need to "put away childish things." A six-year-old's reading of the Scriptures does not ring with authenticity through the voice of a forty-year-old. Still, the sounds of the Scriptures will not be released with healing and transforming power unless we move not around but through critical readings, and beyond them to renewed appreciation of the Scriptures' visual immediacy, dramatic energy, and analytical sparkle.

Good musicians know musicology and performance technique, but effective performance requires them to enter the music. It is not sufficient to sit on their own shoulders while they are playing, reflecting on the history of music interpretation and second-guessing the choices they are making regarding technique. To borrow a line attributed to Jesus, unless we become like little children, we will find it hard to enter the Commonwealth of God (Mark 10:15). There is a difference between being childish and being childlike. To become as a little child is not to regress. It is to reconnect with our heritage as *imago dei—homo ludens*. To find the fire of love that dances and crackles through the Scriptures, and in that energy and Spirit, to play that fire.

Playing the consuming fire, burning bush, and fiery furnace in counterpoint may foster fresh energy in our spiritual imaginations as preachers. Specifically, let's think of those fires in the context of the

24

tender, terrifying dimension of proclamation that cannot be conveyed by simply tagging it "our call to preach." However you have experienced and might describe your own call, I'll bet it hasn't been an easy ride. More likely it has been a conflicted, confusing, paradoxical back-and-forth: thought and feeling, conversation and reflection, insight and confusion, three steps forward, two steps back, sometimes a sidetrack. It has been quite a journey, hasn't it? One in which the God you have encountered has seemed at times all-consuming. One in which you have sometimes felt the fire of God's love accompanying, even preserving you in the fires of adversity. One in which you have not been consumed. (After all, here you are.)

So, at a respectful distance, let's join Moses in the wilderness—a wilderness in more than one sense: not just a forbidding landscape, also a barren heartscape. Back and forth Moses trudges. He has recently undergone a career change—not a promotion, or even a lateral move. Vocationally, he has, it seems, lost everything. Back and forth he wanders, sheep in tow, questioning the leadership skills he exhibited in his previous life. "Should I have killed the Egyptian, or not? Damned if I did, damned if I didn't."

On the far side of a hill stands a little bush. One of hundreds—nondescript. How many times in his wilderness crossings has he passed this little bush? Does he even know? He's hasn't been paying attention. This time, however, the bush blazes with light. Spontaneous combustion, surely. In seconds it will be cinders for desert winds to scatter. Except it doesn't disintegrate. Engulfed in flames, its branches and leaves seem more alive than any he has ever seen. "How can that be? I must go see!" Off Moses ambles toward the burning bush. Coming upon it he hears a voice. Bass—alto—lyric soprano? Your guess is as good as mine. But what the voice says is unmistakable: "Lose the shoes!" The place Moses shares with the burning bush is sacred space, apparently. How was *he* supposed to know, for goodness' sake?

Let's keep playing with this splendid text—with all due respect,

25

and a twinkle in the eye. That is one way we, along with Moses, can render homage to the Presence who chooses to become palpable in the dancing flames.

A burning bush on the landscape of the desert—landscape and desert in more ways than one. In the not-too-distant past, Moses was a prince in Egypt. If you had asked him then to describe his station in life (or his sense of himself) with reference to some form of plant, what do you suppose he would have responded? A mighty oak? A stately cedar? How does he imagine himself now? As a scrub is a good guess. A burned-up, burned-out bush. "I beg to differ," Consuming Fire tells him. "You are but a bush; yet one alight with Who I Am. A bush that burns and yet is not consumed."

Perhaps you and I are bushes, as well. Or, to slightly shift the angle of the metaphor, perhaps we encounter any number of bushes, seemingly ordinary features on the terrain of our experience. Nothing about them draws special attention. They are just there, facts of life. Poet Gerard Manley Hopkins talks of "inscape," the essence or "thisness" of things. Maybe it makes sense to talk of daily stuff as various and sundry bushes on the heartscapes of our lives.

Nothing special, these. But how do they or how might they look when set alight by sacred fire? What might be some of the burning bushes on the heartscapes of our experience? What of God's creativity is at work in your call? What of your ordinary experiences has God lit up (or might God light up) in extraordinary ways? Leaving them what they are, yet making of them something new. Burning them without consuming them. God at work within you, playing with fire.

"Who am I, that I should preach?" we ask, in vigorous, honest protest. God, I suspect, honors that question in a way we could scarcely imagine—by returning it to us with total seriousness: "Who are you, that you should preach? Who, indeed? Take a careful look and listen, and tell me what you come upon! Having put those pieces there, allowed them there, or met you in the midst of them, I have a fair sense of who you already are and can become!"

"The first law of the spiritual life is attention," I once heard Alan Jones say to seminarians during a retreat. When we look at the heartscapes of our lives, what do we see? What do we hear? What do we touch? (Asking those questions is not the same as asking, How good do we look? How good do we sound? How fit are we for the preaching life?)

We need to pay attention as best we can to the primary, immediate tones and textures of our experiences, because somewhere within them the fire of God already burns, or one day will. Do not worry in the least that such attentiveness will lead you down a self-absorbing path into the depths of pulpit narcissism (expounding, "Let me tell you what this passage of the Scriptures means to me in my own personal life"). It shouldn't, and, properly undertaken, it won't. Preaching is not about us. But it happens only through us. At the very least, none of us can preach save through the baritone or mezzo-soprano voice we have been given—along with its distinctive accent, its particular play of vocabulary and syntax, its very own reservoir of discrete experiences.

"We preach not ourselves, but Christ, and him crucified. And our selves as your servants for Jesus' sake" (2 Cor 4:5). Well, yes, Saint Paul says it right. But do you notice how utterly Pauline he is, every time he opens his mouth and utters a phrase? He can't help it. How he preaches is inseparable from who he is. It is his distinctive way of living out the idea that *imago dei*—*homo ludens*. It is how Paul plays with fire—in no small measure marked by the ways God has lit all sorts of burning bushes on the heartscape of Paul's experience. Yet it is not uniquely Paul's. The same thing happens with every other chosen vessel God first touches with fire and then tells to pass it on.

Think of the vast array of preaching styles we'd hear if the authors and characters of the Scriptures could share their sermons with us live! All you have to do is trace some of the features of their proclamation texts to get a sense of what different sorts of fire are kindled

27

through the play of various artists. Can you imagine Jeremiah preaching sermons that sound just like Nehemiah's? Would Esther come across as indistinguishable from Ruth? Peter's way with words is rather different from Paul's, is it not? From what we know of them, could we infer that Mary and Mary Magdalene would proclaim the story of the Resurrection in unison? Highly doubtful, don't you think?

Let's dwell a bit with the Jesus we see and hear, courtesy of the four Evangelists. The Jesus of Matthew's Gospel sounds to me like a wise, discerning mentor, helping newly minted disciples make clear, hard choices between elements "old and new" that can by no means be equated with, or easily identified as, bad and good.

Luke, by tradition a physician and by textual evidence a skilled rhetorician, rings change after change of answers to the inextricably interconnected questions "How is healing heard?" and "How is hearing healed?" His answer involves all sorts of literary genres—notably preaching by singing. And many of the most epiphany-igniting lines in Luke's Gospel are given not to Jesus, but to a wide variety of testifying voices—male and female, human and angel, Jew and Roman, rich and poor (all of whom, incidentally, even in the short lines they are given, manifest clearly their way with God's word). God lights up the ordinary vocational skills of Saint Luke in ways that give you glimpses of burning bushes on the heartscapes of all kinds of people.

John's Jesus is a conceptual iconographer. He has long discussions about complex metaphysical issues—charged with vivid, graphic fireworks ("born again," "living water," "bread of life," "true vine," and "good shepherd," to name a few). Folks like Nicodemus and the woman at the well are seriously engaged—and utterly bewildered—by a Jesus who seems bent on plunging them beneath the settled surfaces of their lives into the wild expanse of eternal life. To encounter Jesus in John's Gospel is to be upended by the vertigo of grace.

Mark's Jesus is the impulsive, explosive, compassionate insurgent, constantly silencing demons through strategic words and exercising authority through immediate moves. And then, after his execution for being the system-threatening invader that he is, Mark's Jesus addresses the fears of his followers by shifting stones, and running on ahead of them with an urgent, over-the-shoulder summons: "Follow me." Your tongue hangs out and your eyes get wide when you try to follow Jesus by listening to Mark's preaching voice. No stirring charge ("Go ye therefore and preach the Gospel to all nations")—that's Matthew. No patient words of healing along the Emmaus road—that's Luke. No "Peace be with you," followed by a Spirit breathing—for that you must to listen to John.

Imagine the different experiences in the lives of each author (and the formidable problems in each author's congregations) that God has to light up in order to produce this breathtaking Gospel fireworks display! Ordinary experiences, touched by fire. Fuel for glorious, inextinguishable burning. Preachers, all of these, burning, but not consumed. Producing play that expresses and evokes freedom, community, adventure, creativity. Gospel writers, each distinctively playing with fire.

If we do our homework, paying attention with care, sorting through treasures hidden in our own fields, surveying our heartscapes for burning bushes, we will become more proficient in our attempts to hear, see, taste, touch, and feel what is going on in the Scriptures as well. We will gain a more acute sense of how we can begin to interpret biblical texts—not as external observers, but as participating players in the experience of amazing grace. This is not a covert way of suggesting that Scripture passages are Rorschach blots on which to impose our personal projections. We can see what is going on for characters in and authors of the Scriptures, not because we know just how they feel (how silly!), not because we know everything about the biblical texts, but rather because we can see something of what a biblical text can be about.

So where do we start in search of fire? How does the spiritual discipline of listening for the sound of a call to preach inform our investigation? We can look, listen, touch, taste, and even alert our nostrils to the scent of experiences—discrete and in clusters, ready to hand and held in memory, shared and solitary—experiences that mark us as particular players in the order of God's creation. We are not looking for what makes us special, in the sense of being more qualified than others (as certified by successful competition with them). What we discover, and offer for God's service, will not be so unique that it has no conceivable point of contact with another's discovery. What is in each of us—an interplay of personal factors that cannot be replicated—will, instead, serve as a place of meeting with others. What is universal in human experiences is never generic. Connection with another (and with the Other) occurs always and only by bringing personal distinctiveness into places of shared discovery. What we hold in common is uncommon Mystery.

I suspect that proclamations of the Gospel sometimes fall flat because they are cast in the form of abstract absolutes, issued to whom it may concern, delivered by no one in particular. The Scriptures themselves rigorously resist our efforts so to cast them. And God tends to get impatient (and even to break out) when passed off as simply the Ground of Being.

So, then, who are we that we should preach? What are the burning bushes to which we will do well to pay attention? The attempt to honor God's revelatory gifts in our own experience can be pursued as a discerning discipline of spiritual exercises. My earlier book *Your Way with God's Word: Discovering Your Distinctive Preaching Voice* presents a framework of space-shaping invitations for personal reflection to be conducted, ideally, not in private but in conversation with other preachers. (The most effective way to discern how you sound distinctively is to participate in lively collegial interchange.) Let me pique your interest in such an undertaking by reviewing and slightly recasting the dimensions of self-discovery that the exercises in that book seek to prompt:

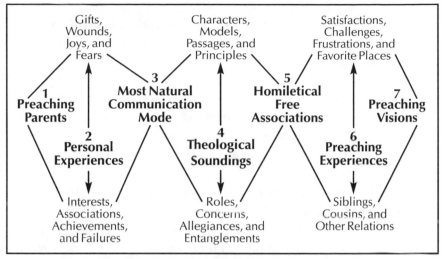

Figure 1: The dimensions of a preacher's journey of self-discovery

1. *Whom we have come from.* Recalling the particular legacies of our own preaching parents—not our homiletics professors, but those whose sermons formed our first feelings for what it means to hear and speak the Gospel.

2. *What we have been up to.* Recounting some conditioning "givens" and important events that have happened to us, and the wide sweep of things we have done.

3. *How we make sense.* Reflecting on the ways we shape and share our experiences—whether we process and communicate primarily in the language of images, stories, or ideas.

4. *When we say "AMEN!"* Rehearsing various personalities, principles, and passages from the Scriptures and Christian tradition with which we find ourselves in deep and centering resonance.

5. *What our preaching can be compared with.* Reviewing concrete physical objects and activities that seem somehow—regardless of how improbably—associated, analogically or metaphorically, with preaching as we do it.

6. *Where we fit, and with whom.* Ruminating on the comfort zones in our preaching, and the nurturing presences who give us growing space.
7. *Why we really care.* Reaffirming the deeply felt sense of personal vocation that we would like to be able to offer as a liberating legacy to those for whom we have become preaching parents.

The unfolding adventure of that discernment journey is mapped in figure 1.

In working with preaching colleagues, I have found that aspects of experience identified through each of those lenses enter into fascinating interplay with each other. If not clearly identified, the interacting factors can significantly inhibit a preacher's growth. I am thinking, for instance, of a young man who was exceptionally gifted in his ability to paint spiritually illuminating verbal pictures. He was, however, when first we began talking, close to despair about whether he could ever really learn to preach. His preaching parent, his parish pastor during his early years in church, had preached primarily by concepts, analytic paragraphs, and propositions. Once that issue had been named, it was not difficult for my friend to recognize that he neither could nor should preach just like his "dad." He turned his attention, then, to evoking in his own listeners, in his own way, a hearing of the Gospel that was analogous, but not identical, to the hearing that his formative pastor had evoked in him.

No two preachers are clones (at least no two authentic and effective preachers are). No one kindles fire exactly as another does (indeed, no one person ever strikes two effective sermons in an identical fashion). This might seem to indicate that preachers have nothing to offer each other as professional colleagues ("You do it your way, I'll do it mine—God bless us, every one!"). But that is not correct.

It is true that neither you nor I can prepare and preach each other's sermons. But we can, with careful attention and due respect to the distinctiveness of each other's ways, learn from and give valuable help to one another. The more clearly I hear you, the more clearly I become aware of our similarities and differences. I can appropriate your strengths in my own way. Hearing firsthand some of the costs involved in how I preach, you can get a better feel for what might be limitations in your own style and approach—and what you might do to compensate for those. Competition with you, born of my own insecurity, is simply unnecessary. There are many members in the One Body, each having different gifts—none of whom can say to another, "I have no need of thee."

In the next stages of this adventure, I shall suggest a metalanguage for healthy collegial interchange—a professional vocabulary we can use to listen to and talk about our own preaching and that of our colleagues in ways that are discerning and evocative, rather than vaguely abstract or unhelpfully judgmental. But before we move ahead to that stage of the journey, it is worth lingering here a bit longer to observe that, even though no two preachers (or sermons) are alike, they bear certain family resemblances. Particular colleagues may share specific, discrete ways of giving shape to the sound of amazing grace. I may find myself more at home, in some respects, with the folks who live across the street than with the people who surrounded me when I grew up. The colleague I just mentioned fit in better with picture-painting colleagues than with his former pastor.

What might distinctive preaching types look like? Let me proffer some suggestions—a spreadsheet of sorts, set forth as a series of caricatures (see figure 2). I have used caricatures not to belittle any of the types, but to emphasize distinctive features so that as we survey the types, we can reflect on potential points of identification. As you look at figure 2, ask yourself, "Who am I most like, least like, somewhat like, sometimes like?" Look at or listen to a sampling of sermons you have preached. Or simply sit and think about how you read the Scriptures, observe and reflect on life, and shape and share the sermons that arise from within you. Where on the list do you come closest to seeing and hearing yourself?

The spectrum in figure 2 is only suggestive. There may well be other types, and subsets of types. You won't fit neatly into any one of the categories. No preacher does. Nevertheless, there is a certain value in characterizations based on these categories—like the initial descriptions we offer as we introduce ourselves to others. They are not the truth, the whole truth, and nothing but the truth, but places to start, meeting places for conversation.

This way of envisioning different preaching voices may help us move beyond the obvious observation that every preacher is different. If Jeremiah and Nehemiah have distinctive voices, perhaps that distinction can be further clarified by noting that the former often operates in censure mode, whereas the latter partakes much more of

Sermon type	Pulpit space	Primary purpose	Catalyst for transformation	Informing flavor
Lecture	Classroom	Inform	Feed intellect	"This you need to know!"
Censure	Principal's office	Correct	Change will	"Clean up your act, or else."
Pep talk	Locker room	Inspire	Rouse feelings	"You can do it!"
Hug	Hospital/ therapy couch	Heal	Bind wounds	"It's going to be all right."
Sales pitch	Marketplace/ shopping mall	Attract	Generate interest	"This you cannot live without!"
Reflection	Retreat center	Refocus/ reframe	Shift imagination	"Might it be that…"
Legal defense	Courtroom	Convince	Prove case	"The evidence demands a verdict!"
Confession	Alcoholics Anonymous meeting	Release	Share weakness	"I'm X, a forgiven sinner—who are you?"
Cheer	Backyard/ banquet hall	Celebrate	Kindle joy	"God is awesome; this is great!"

Figure 2: Preaching parents: a gallery of caricatures

the pep-talk and sales-pitch ways of speaking. What do you think about other distinctive Scripture voices? Some texts nestle easily into certain categories, and can't be squeezed into others. Psalms of praise are designed for celebrations, and yet I have heard preachers with distinctive censure voices override the natural voices of the texts. Psalm 100 can be proclaimed so as to make listeners feel guilty for praise they haven't offered! If interpreters like Walter Brueggemann are right, Psalm 100 can be heard as a pep talk—or, to put it more elegantly, as a ringing affirmation regarding which God is God, and which gods are not (see *Israel's Praise: Doxology Against Idolatry and Ideology*, Philadelphia: Fortress Press, 1988).

Which kind of preaching voice is best? To raise the question is to hear how silly it sounds—a question, as the Buddha says, "that tends not to edification." At different times for different purposes, God uses different voices. But seldom in the same sermon!

One of the impressions that may have hit you as you sat with the caricature spreadsheet is how perfectly terrible certain lecture, hug, confession, or reflection preaching has sounded in your ear! "If I ever get put in a pulpit, that is the one kind of preacher I will never be!" you may have muttered under your breath as you listened to that preaching and stole furtive glances at your watch. Every type of preaching voice can be poorly, even horrendously represented. But each type can also sound forth with rich and graceful power.

It is never the case, however, that preachers are just fine just the way they are. All preachers are called to stretch and grow. But unless we are clearly called by God (not by feelings of guilt or envy) to develop a different voice, our improvement comes by way of growing clarity as to the particular possibilities and limitations of our particular gifts.

Growth occasioned by nurture and challenge is essential in a preaching life. Additional experience brings additional richness, variety—and, sooner or later, a restless sense of the need to get on with it. However, the objective of that developmental trajectory is not simply to garner a vast store of voicing options from which to pull out new sounds that shake up our listeners. Indeed, we are often more effective as our listeners become more familiar with how we sound.

Sacred fire will consume only what needs burning off, so that what remains can burn more brightly still. Being consumed by the fire of God means being caught up in it, but never destroyed by it. Have you not found this so as you have tried to preach?

"Who am I that I should preach?" is not a question answered easily or all at once. God takes that perfectly understandable rhetorical question and bounces it back in our direction with literal force: "Who, indeed? Search your heartscape and say what you see!" Burning bushes blaze up in places unanticipated and unexpected. When our attention is arrested, we go closer. Like Moses, we are invited onto holy ground. Admonished, admittedly, to keep a reverent distance, we are not invited (or allowed) to leave. Standing in such a space, we are well advised to lose our shoes.

4

Open My Servant's Eyes

When an attendant of the man of God rose early in the morning and went out, an army with horses and chariots was all around the city. His servant said, "Alas, master! What shall we do?" He replied, "Do not be afraid, for there are more with us than there are with them." Then Elisha prayed: "O Lord, please open his eyes that he may see." So the Lord opened the eyes of the servant, and he saw; the mountain was full of horses and chariots of fire all around Elisha. (2 Kings 6:15–17)

How can a preacher play with fire? So far our concern has been more vocational than technical: "How do we dare?" rather than "How do we begin?" No skill set can substitute for a preacher's sense of call. Becoming a preacher involves mystery that is not reducible to strategies employed in doing the job. Yet technical mastery is not devoid of mystery. Sometimes you study, pray, scribble, and click, but the sermon remains beyond reach. Sometimes, having shouldered the same discipline, you sense, "I've got something!" and the eyes of listeners say that they beg to differ. Sometimes you don't have time or energy to get it together, but holy fire descends on the altar of your sermon anyway, transforming your words, your listeners, and even you. Sometimes some folks get it and others don't. And once in a while someone thanks you for something you know you didn't say.

Both in calling and in crafting there is mystery—that upon which we can never gain full purchase because we are immersed within it. The more clarity we achieve, the more aware we become of the vast expanse beyond our grasp. Yet what we can't encompass we can still address. What methods can we employ to help us do the job?

The challenge in making any suggestions about preaching strategy is to evoke in different preachers who work in different settings a feel for the preaching art that they share in common. It is not difficult in the abstract to name steps, virtues, and underlying principles, and even to give examples that prompt preaching students to say, "I get it!" But such flashes of insight are often short lived or mechanically applied. Why is it so hard to get it, and why is it so hard to help? Because the move from instruction to education is especially problematic when all involved are attempting to become reflective practitioners, making use of principles that never apply exactly the same way twice. Daunting work, indeed!

So let's consider the serious business of preaching as an exercise of spirit play. In chapter 2, we noted the wide range of activities that count as play. From the richness of this notion I think we can discern certain features that preachers can internalize, features that can serve as illuminating, energizing centers in two related dimensions of sermon-shaping artistry. A clearly articulated sense of what it means to play can foster fire in these areas:

• Three stages through which all preaching preparation needs to move
• Three strategies that all preachers need to employ in that process

We designate as play specific activities that serve as occasions of freedom, community, adventure, and creativity (we play cards, clarinets, soccer, the role of Lady Macbeth). We also use play to describe certain ways of going about our activities—whether or not the activities themselves are named as play (we play with our keys, our schedules, our options). Three playful ways of going about whatever we do are viscerally analogous to the three successive stages in effective sermon preparation:

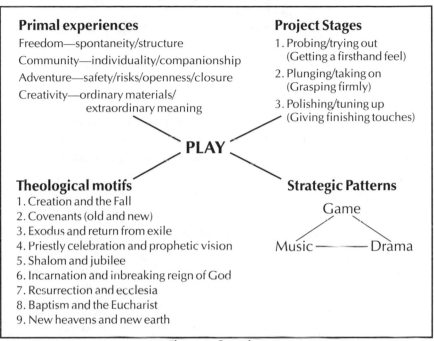

Primal experiences
Freedom—spontaneity/structure
Community—individuality/companionship
Adventure—safety/risks/openness/closure
Creativity—ordinary materials/
extraordinary meaning

Project Stages
1. Probing/trying out
(Getting a firsthand feel)
2. Plunging/taking on
(Grasping firmly)
3. Polishing/tuning up
(Giving finishing touches)

PLAY

Theological motifs
1. Creation and the Fall
2. Covenants (old and new)
3. Exodus and return from exile
4. Priestly celebration and prophetic vision
5. Shalom and jubilee
6. Incarnation and inbreaking reign of God
7. Resurrection and ecclesia
8. Baptism and the Eucharist
9. New heavens and new earth

Strategic Patterns
Game
Music ———— Drama

Figure 3. Overview

1. When a child (of any age) receives a demonstration of a new toy or tool, she or he will often demand, "Let me play with it!" Such an insistence expresses the desire for a secondhand experience to be transcended by a firsthand feel. To play can mean to get in touch with something for oneself; this is *trying-out* play.

2. Often, after a group has been playing around at an activity for a while, a call goes out: "Come on! Let's really play!" That is an invitation (or a challenge) to move from getting acquainted with to getting serious about. Play around the edges of an activity, though an entry point, cannot continue indefinitely. Participants must move from trying out to plunging in—from getting a firsthand feel to grasping firmly with both hands. If they don't, the activity tends to wind down. A move from entry to immersion intensifies energy.

So to play can mean not just to explore tentatively but also to enter fully, with passion, concentration, even sweat! This type of play could look like work, but it doesn't feel that way because everyone is having so much fun; it is *taking-on* play.

3. When artists (say, painters or poets) approach the end of their creative process, they often resist turning loose what they are working with: "Not just yet! It isn't done! I need to play with it a little more!" Such play involves pruning, polishing, and adding finishing touches to what has been worked over or played with lovingly and for so long. To play thus means to alternate between stepping back for perspective and reengaging at close range for further perfecting; this is *tuning-up* play.

Figure 3 illustrates the connection between these three ways of playing, and the three-staged sequence of movement and momentum that unfolds in sermon preparation. The order cannot be short cut or subverted (although one may need to drop back to an earlier stage before moving ahead). Preachers sometimes have weeks in which to prepare sermons, sometimes only hours or even minutes. Regardless, these stages need to be played out in sequence.

The following chart sketches broadly the questions addressed at each stage of the process.

Stages in the Play of Preaching Preparation: A Brief Overview

1. Probing Play / Trying-out Play (Soft Focus)
    - What catches my eye, my ear, my heart in the Scripture text—especially in light of congregational, cultural, liturgical, and personal dynamics that are currently at play?
    - What catches my attention when the text is brought into play with biblical, historical, and theological factors that surround and influence it?

2. Plunging Play/Taking-on Play (Sharp Focus)
   - What understandings concerning these various voices do I need in order to make the preaching conversation live—to give it both energy and integrity?
   - What resources are important for gaining those understandings?
   - What plot flow or unfolding dynamic thrust suggests itself in light of this progressively deepening, progressively more animated conversation?
   - What primary rhetorical strategy—image, story, or argument—suggests itself as best suited for taking listeners directly into this flow and thrust?
   - How might other strategies be orchestrated to support the primary one?
3. Polishing Play/Tuning-up Play (Synergizing Focus)
   - What moves in the trial plot flow are extraneous or have been left out?
   - What details in the description or explanation need fleshing up or pruning down?
   - How can the sermon's plot elements be sharpened and energized?
   - How can the language be made more immediate (less distant or abstract)?
   - How can the sermon flow be made more engaging (speaking for and with its listeners, rather than around, about, or at them)?

In the next two chapters, we will focus on stages 2 and 3. Now let's zero in on stage 1 play, where we try out ideas and get a firsthand feel for where the sermon might go.

A story in 2 Kings, chapter 6, suggests what we are about here. Elisha, the prophet, has been (or so it seems) eavesdropping from a distance on the war plans of the king of Aram. Elisha anticipates the military moves of the Arameans "more than once or twice," and sends advance word of the targets to the king of Israel. Forewarned, the king of Israel is forearmed; the raids are repelled.

Aram's king is less than pleased. "Now tell me who among us sides with the king of Israel?" he demands, addressing a cowering assemblage of underlings. "No one, my lord king," one replies. "It is Elisha, the prophet in Israel, who tells the king of Israel the words that you speak in your own bedchamber." "Go and find where he is; I will send and seize him," the leader thunders. The first part of that order poses no problem: Elisha is discovered in Dothan. Dispatching horses and chariots to Dothan is also easy (the king has plenty of both). The seizing part turns out to be more difficult. Elisha's attendant awakens to find the city surrounded by overwhelming force. He reports his alarming observation to the prophet: "Alas, master! What shall we do?" Elisha is unconcerned: "Do not be afraid," he says, "for there are more with us than there are with them." Knowing this will be hard for the terrified attendant to take on faith, Elisha sends up a prayer: "O LORD, open his eyes, that he may see." God does just that, the storyteller says: "The LORD opened the eyes of the servant, and he saw; the mountain was full of horses and chariots of fire all around Elisha."

Elisha refuses to take advantage of his superior firepower. The raiding party is inflicted with temporary blindness and led to the door of the king of Israel, who asks permission to slay the whole troop. Elisha counsels a different strategy: feed them and send them home. Foolishness! Such kindness will be interpreted as weakness, and will only exacerbate the aggression of the king of Aram! But the storyteller says that after the king of Israel follows Elisha's advice, "the Arameans no longer came raiding into the land of Israel." Food offered to enemy soldiers turns out to be food for thought for the cynical servants of Realpolitik who can summon the courage to taste and see!

"A likely story! Quaint mythology!" some might say. "That was then, but this is now!" others might chorus. "But this has nothing to do with preaching," all might well conclude. It all depends, I think, on how you see it. I was drafting this as the horses and chariots of this generation were making final preparations for war against Iraq. Those maneuvers have imperiled more than just the innocent people unfortunate enough to be part of a country that our nation's president has summarily characterized as part of an axis of evil. At profound risk, in many ways, remain all the citizens of the world. What resources has a mere preacher to contend with such firepower? None whatsoever—unless, perhaps, there is time-release potential in Elisha's prayer.

Perhaps, in circumstances such as ours, the resources available to preachers are where (like Elisha's servant) they aren't looking. What if, in a soft-focus scan, with peripheral vision, we could discern, on the horizon of our sacred tradition, some horses and chariots of fire as strategic for our day as Elisha's were for his?

What has this play with a Scripture text to do with the initial stages of preparation for a sermon? Against the forces of spiritual apathy, political arrogance, consumer greed, and militaristic might, the need of the hour is for something to serve as a counterpoint. Unfortunately, a great deal of preaching plunders biblical texts in search of points to be propounded, proved, and then rendered palatable by way of illustration. Maybe, if we are lucky, listeners will take our point rather than the other side's. What preachers often fail to do, however, is allow themselves to be attracted, in subtle, unexpected ways, by the pulsing energy of God on the move across the pages of the Scriptures. We want (and in some respects need) to get to the point of a biblical text, so that we get to the point of the sermon. Nobody is engaged by a sermon that wanders aimlessly, beating around the bush. And yet the well-intended results of our searches for a deliberate point can be disastrous.

I once worked with a preacher who had great difficulty keeping the eyes of his listeners from glazing over. It was not for want of intelligence, or lack of time and effort. After numerous self-confessed (and community-confirmed) sermon failures, he expressed his frustration and disclosed (with pride) his technique: "I don't understand why my sermons don't work," he said. "The first thing I always do is read the text, over and over, until I figure out the doctrine that the passage teaches. Then I write a sermon to explain it." What he was proud of was, in fact, his problem. He always had a point. Period.

But if the Holy Scriptures are a witness to the living God, then points, as such, cannot but misrepresent the sight and sound and feel of what they present. God's pillar of fire is not a point. Pentecost is not a point. Try asking those who quaked with fear before the fire on the mountain: "Tell us, what, exactly, was the point that Yahweh was making here?" Ask Elisha's servant where or what was the point in chariots of fire.

In England, the punctuation mark, the point, that Americans call a period, is referred to as a full stop. When does a dynamic God ever come to that? Perhaps we can, by some form of study akin to stop-action photography, abstract for purposes of analysis an artificial freeze-frame. But let us not mislead ourselves into thinking that God is caught in any static pictures we happen to take. Perhaps we can gesture toward God in terms of certain pulsing, dancing, energy points. Perhaps we can trace the trajectory of God's lightning, as it flashes from west to east. But a still life is hardly appropriate for depicting the God who, across the pages of the Scriptures, is forever showing up as fire! When we render God theologically in terms of formal portrait poses, something is wrong with our pictures! The supposedly immutable God is always on the move.

One challenge for preachers is how to make the biblical texts interesting (after all, they depict issues and events from long ago and faraway). Much careful, critical work is required to release the full energy of ancient texts, of course. But the problem, I submit, is not with the texts themselves (they are almost always faithful to the divine dynamism, regardless of their genre). The problem is the preacher's expectation that biblical texts teach a set, solid truth, whereas instead

44

they sweep their listeners up into a breathtaking, world-upending adventure. To enter any text of the Scriptures is to sign on for a wild ride. A biblical text is like a drama script, a music score, or a playbook. What you look at on the page is a set of notations just waiting to be released in movement, sound, and action.

How can we access the energy of biblical texts in the initial stage of preparing to preach? We can pray for wide eyes. We can scan the horizon for chariots of fire. We can make ourselves available to be caught up in the action. We can ask the primal questions "What in God's name is going on here?" and "Where might this be taking us?"

That may seem a bit difficult to undertake as a deliberate strategy. So let me set down some suggestions for alerting our awareness to the all-surrounding Word. Any number of strategies can be employed, individually and in combination, to help us probe a biblical text, not from an objective distance, but with a firsthand feel.

At first appearance, my suggestions may appear to outline a list-of-rules approach to preaching. But more is involved here, I think—and less. These are not so much steps that we must trace and retrace as they are windows that we may open. Some strategies will work more effectively with certain texts than with others. We will not, in the preparation of a single sermon, undertake them all, investing equal time on each. But here they are. Try some out. What you encounter may all but take your breath away. You may just find, instead of flat, fixed principles, needing to be rendered relevant, dancing sparks, even wholesale outbreaks of sacred fire.

Strategies for Alerting Your Awareness to the All-Surrounding Word

How can you position yourself, in reading the Scriptures, to be attentive—not to points and propositions, issues and concepts, but rather to the action of God, and to the unfolding interactions be-

45

tween God and God's people that are the underlying energy in a biblical text?

1. Read the text aloud. If possible, proclaim it in dramatic dialogue with a small group of readers (which is not the same as taking turns reading verses).

2. Do the same thing in several translations. This will return the text to the medium in which it was first prepared and encountered— whether as a hymn sung in worship, a story recounted to a community, or a letter read to a waiting congregation. The written form is secondary, the oral form is primary. Don't treat the Scriptures as a secondary source!

3. Now try out different interpretive readings—different tones of voice, inflections, phrasings, and so on. What difference does it make to the hearing if the sound is earnest? Angry? Ironic? Pleading? Compassionate? Probing? Cooperative? Contentious?

4. Ask the text some hard questions. Don't ask questions that are rhetorical, questions that will allow for only quick, easy answers, or even questions of exegetical context—at least, not yet. Instead, ask questions that court tension, ambiguity, and a sense of imbalance. Approach the text not with beady theological eyes, but with a soft focus, prepared to turn your gaze toward movements in your peripheral vision.

5. In response to what you see and hear, talk back to the text, posing questions such as the ones that follow:
   - "What's this?" (When you see something curious, perplexing, seemingly irrelevant, utterly mundane, rather off-putting, very unsettling, or even downright sacrilegious.)
   - "That's crazy!" (When what you are reading about doesn't seem to fit into the bigger biblical picture in which it occurs. When it seems out of sync with what everybody—especially pious bodies!—knows about religion.)
   - "Yes, but . . ." (When what meets the eye makes a certain

46

amount of sense—but, on the other hand, surely doesn't seem to be the whole truth, and nothing but the truth, about what we experience.)

- "What's at stake here?" (When the writer, or a character portrayed by the writer, is clearly exercised about what is being said.)

6. Now step back and try to get a bigger picture, asking questions like these:
   - "Where did this come from?" (What, in this book or in previous biblical history or writings, is the preliminary act that this particular scene is reacting to or extending?)
   - "Then what happens?" (What, in this book or in subsequent biblical history or writings, is the subsequent scene, reaction, or string of unfolding events?)
   - "Where is this taking us?" (Where are we hanging when the reading leaves off? What has been resolved? What remains to be resolved? What things seemingly resolved before have been undone by this? What implications seem to follow?)

7. Finally, look for jars and sparks—places of dissonance and resonance with things outside the text:
   - with other biblical texts
   - with what is going on in your community (local, national, international, congregational)
   - with what else is taking place in the liturgy of the day
   - with circumstances in your personal life
   - with issues in the culture at large
   - with assertions and affirmations from Christian tradition, and from ecclesial communities and institutions

In summary: Do not look for the point, the period, the full stop. Look for the question mark, the exclamation point, the comma, or the semicolon. Look for the knot, the arrow, the clash, the stretch, and the spark.

47

All the suggestions offered in the preceding chart can be integrated into a sequential set of soft-focus readings of the lessons appointed in the lectionary for a given occasion:

1. *Beginning to end.* An "out loud/acting out" reading of and movement through the lesson as assigned. This reading focuses on what catches attention, what moves, what jangles. It is an attempt to access the immediate energy awaiting release in the score or script. It opens awareness to the sense of the text—in all senses of the term *sense*.

2. *Before and after.* A broader, "dynamic framing" of the scene or section that will be read from the lectern at the service of public worship. This reading moves, in a series of brief stages, behind and ahead of the text. It is an attempt to hear, see, and feel the narrative flow through which the text emerges. It opens awareness to the sweep of sacred energy in which the text participates.

3. *Back and forth.* A comparative reading of the passage (especially if the passage is a Gospel) with biblical parallels. This reading seeks to discover what is distinctive about the text under exploration. It is an attempt to discern the voicing nuance of this text's author. It opens awareness to the slant—the particular angle, tone, or color of sacred artistry—in the Scriptures.

4. *Around and under.* A gentle scanning of other lections appointed for the day (in their immediate contexts). This reading seeks to ascertain possible illuminating "deep structure" dynamics. It is an attempt not to pin down themes, but to listen for covenantal resonance. It opens awareness to sparks of analogous Sacred Fire alight in other times and places in the history of God's pilgrim people.

These readings need to be undertaken *before* you make the connections named in the seventh strategy for alerting your awareness. Otherwise the integrity, potential freshness, idiosyncrasy, and dynamic relevance (as opposed to superficial similarities of "topic," "issue," or "theme") may arise as authentic voices for interplay in the larger Spirit-ed conversation.

What you are doing in all of this, rather than trying to get the point, is positioning yourself to be surprised. A soft focus will facilitate peripheral vision, which, in time, will generate a double take. When you catch your breath and say, almost involuntarily (and all but literally), "Oh, God!" you are probably close to the energy in the text—an energy that will almost certainly take you on a wild ride, a Gospel frolic.

In his book *The Sermon: Dancing the Edge of Mystery*, Eugene L. Lowry suggests the following additional and complementary strategies for staying open to the richness and energy of a biblical text. Try, says Lowry, to get "out of control":

- Look for trouble, for what is unsettling, weird, or "up in the air." Look for anything that forestalls closure that seems to court disaster.
- Position yourself to be surprised in relation to characters in the text (identify with someone whose position is alien to your own).
- Role play the text with others.
- Talk out loud with others about the text.
- Paraphrase the text.
- Ask what assumptions you are bringing to the text.
- Look for a different angle from which to approach a familiar landing field (a different chord structure that might underlie a familiar melody).
- Identify any clear images that are present in the text, or which the text triggers in your consciousness.
- Note the actions, and the unresolved tensions in the text.
- Trace the back-and-forth of dialogue in the text, what seems left unsaid, what is being said between the lines.

- Underline everything that you think is important in the text; then go back and look at what is left.
- Name the numerous unresolved issues, the hanging questions. Name what seems to be most at stake. Then look for the turn of the text (something that could not be easily anticipated, but, in a surprising way, makes deep sense).

(Nashville: Abingdon Press, 1997;

see especially chapter 5)

Reasonably enough, the eyes of the attendant of Elisha were firmly fixed on the problem right in front of him. That made it impossible for him to see where the action was. Firmly fixed visions have a way of keeping us from seeing what is going on around us! The action of God, the illuminating, protecting, cleansing, transforming fire, is often a part of the picture already—but more available to soft-focus perception at the periphery of consciousness than at the point where one happens to be staring.

I know a preacher who was facing a serious financial crisis in his parish—low membership, low contributions, and high expenses because of long-deferred maintenance to the building. The text appointed from the lectionary was from Acts of the Apostles, chapter 8, the story of Philip's encounter with the Ethiopian eunuch. The preacher wasn't making much progress in preparing a sermon on the reading. He decided to try the second-to-the-last technique in the list suggested by Lowry. He carefully underlined, in the selected verses, all the words and phrases that seemed to be really important. He then returned to review what was left. To his surprise, he discovered that the word *go* appeared several times over, and that in each case, he had overlooked it. The sermon for his flock on the following Sunday, rather than addressing the discouraging shortfall in parish revenue, was a call to follow the Spirit's leading into a world hungry for a touch of grace.

What we are likely to see, if we open our eyes in the way that

Lowry suggests, is not a quick solution to our quest for a sermon. Quite the contrary. We may find, rather, that the soft-focus, firsthand-feel play with the Scriptures yields far more questions than answers. Rather than quell our preparation anxiety, it may raise the level of tension significantly. However, this is all to the good! It means we have burning issues that, without knowing just how, we know we must confront. That kind of energy is exactly the stuff of which sermons that play with fire are made. This is, after all, only the first stage of preparation—the point of which is not to tie things down, but to open things up. What happens when we approach a biblical text as an adventure on the brink of overtaking us? The image, issue, or action in the text that, consciously or instinctively, we might seek to avoid, since it causes so much friction, becomes the kindling point from which energy, warmth, and light eventually break forth.

Surrender yourself to the energy of a brief sermon that caught fire for its preacher when he scanned the text of the familiar story of the woman at the well in chapter four of John's Gospel. Returning to see what he had left after underlining the important points in the passage, the preacher noted that unrecognized, in the far corner of consciousness, was an irrelevant bit—a water jar. The jar caught the preacher's attention, and here is the sermon that came out:

"Then she left her water jar and went back to the city."
Did you hear that?
She left her water jar!
Look, folks: in Samaria, water is like gold.
It is drawn from deep wells in water jars.
It is hard work.

You would not easily forget a water jar.
Water jars are much too valuable.
Especially if you are a social outcast,

The kind of person who comes to the well at midday.
After all, no one else comes in the heat of the day.

But she left it.
Left it right there and went back to the city!
Why?

She could, perhaps, have forgotten it.
Forgotten it in haste.
Haste to flee the cold stares of the disciples.
(A man and a woman talking together in public.
And a Samaritan woman, at that!
What could Jesus be thinking? Scandal!)

This water jar could have been a gift for Jesus.
After all, he did ask for water.
And he didn't have a jar of his own.

But perhaps she left this jar because she didn't need it
    any more.
She didn't need the ceaseless rounds of drawing water,
Only to come up thirsty again.
Ceaseless rounds . . . drawing water.
The water of lost relationships,
Of attacks on her self-esteem,
Of being an outcast,
Of feeling alone.

Perhaps there was no room left in this jar for Living
    Water.
Perhaps when she had tasted Living Water, the old jar
    seemed to be useless baggage.

And when you are on a mission, you can't be burdened
  by an old water jar.
For she was now a vessel herself.
Full of the Living Water of Jesus.
And it was time to share.

And so our Lord Jesus bids us as well to stop our cease-
  less rounds.
To leave our water jars with him
And taste the Living Water.

Of course, to leave our jars is scary.
They are like gold to us.
They represent a lifetime of hard work!
To some of us, they may be much too valuable just to
  leave behind.
Without them, we might feel like social outcasts.
For these are jars in which we carry our pride,
Our sense of approval,
Our accomplishments, our acquisitions,
Our control.

Perhaps these jars are handy for hiding things.
Things no one else can see.
Things like fear or guilt,
Loneliness or regret,
Grief or shame.

So you have to ask the question:
Are these valuable jars of ours so full
That there is no room for Living Water?

Yet Jesus bids us put the jars down.
"Leave them with me," he says.
"You won't need them, or want them,
After you have tasted Living Water."

Living Water.
Drink out of an old water jar,
And you come up thirsty again.
But not when you drink this stuff!
Living Water becomes in us a spring that gushes eternal
    life!

We will want more than just a taste.
We will want to be submerged in it!
So that our lives can be washed clean, made ready for a
    new beginning,
Buried, so that we can have a share in Christ's Resur-
    rection.

When you are on a mission, you can't be burdened with
    useless baggage.
And old water jars don't seem like much
When you are a vessel for Living Water.
So Jesus bids us leave the jars with him
And go back into the city to share the new life within us.

Praise God for new life
That just doesn't fit into old jars!

("She Left Her Water Jar"
by The Reverend Richmond Webster)

5

Were Not Our Hearts Burning?

When he was at the table with them, he took bread, blessed and broke it,
and gave it to them.

Then their eyes were opened, and they recognized him; and he van-
ished from their sight. They said to each other, "Were not our hearts burn-
ing within us while he was talking to us on the road, while he was opening
the scriptures to us?" That same hour they got up and returned to
Jerusalem; and they found the eleven and their companions gathered to-
gether. (Luke 24:30–33)

No spark, no fire. But sparks alone are not enough. Fires take tending. Think of what it takes to make a campfire. Carefully you position
leaves and twigs (Not too many, not too big! Add them gradually—
but keep them coming!). Gently you blow (a steady, moderate
stream—too soft, the flame will fail; too strong, you'll blow it out!).
The task can be tedious. Kindling a fire is not a rote procedure; it's an
art. Good fire builders don't pause to calculate each move (the flame
would die if they did). Yet their moves are not ad hoc. There is method
in playing with fire. It's work—but fun!

Some preachers shrink from sermon preparation, feeling they
lack skill in finding sparks. Others come up with insights easily enough
but find it hard to tend the sparks. The initial "Aha!" sputters and dies,
smothered by their efforts to fuel it. The research phase of sermon
preparation requires lots of left-brain activity. Even if they employed

a right-brain approach in the first stage of preparation, they find themselves now trudging and slogging, not skipping and dancing.

Yet the work of tending can be fun. What began as playful in stage 1 preparation can become a different form of play. Stage 2 preaching preparation moves us from probing, trying-out, soft-focus play to plunging-in play.

We have already gotten a firsthand feel for what seems alive and alight in the materials we are working with:

- the biblical text (and its various contexts)
- the complex overlay of cultural and community-life textures
- the features of the terrain currently blazing on our own heartscapes
- the other given liturgical elements in the worship service planned for the day

Now we move ahead to take hold with both hands—to really play—with disciplined concentration. The focus of the eye shifts from soft to sharp. What we caught sight of in peripheral vision now moves to the center of attention. Yet sharp focus does not mean fixed staring; the twinkle in the eye can come along. There is, I suggest, a set of specific methods in play throughout the second stage of the kindling art. We undertake the work with energies akin to the particular kinds of fire that we find in games, in music, and in drama.

Preaching as Game

What is engaging about a well-played game? Competition is often an element; but winning isn't everything. Skill, and grace in the moves of players? The artistry in layups or slap shots can all but take the breath away. Single super-stars can stick out like sore thumbs. Carefully coordinated efforts of a whole team, however, those can be mesmerizing. Well-matched opponents, playing cleanly and intensely—it doesn't get any better!

What is at the heart of all this energy? I suggest it's spirited interactivity toward specific objectives. Games are about back and forth, making plays that build on or counter previous moves. The more complex and demanding strategies and counterstrategies become, the higher the energy rises for participants and spectators alike. In a vigorous physical game, spectators lean into the action with empathetic energy. (Watch a Wimbledon tennis match, and see what your body does!).

A volleyball competition with six-foot-tall athletes on one side, and six-year-olds on the other isn't a game. Sometimes preachers (speaking, they presume, on God's behalf) feel it their duty to deliver spikes or to score aces. Perhaps it's not surprising if listeners show scant interest when that is what they are served from the pulpit! For, as figure 4A puts it, effective preaching finds what's already up in the air and passes it back and forth—over and over.

As a preacher, I go to a text of the Scriptures searching for animated discourse, for spirited conversation, for what is at stake, in play between God and God's people, one character and another, author and God, author and audience. "Thus saith the Lord" is never a final word, a "Now hear this—and don't talk back!" Whether consoling, affirming, pleading, warning, or even castigating, God is always making a move—with a high investment in what transpires through the back and forth. If I render "what God says" as a set of static pronouncements, I almost certainly misrepresent the energy of the encounter.

While the Scriptures depict a series of Spirit-ed conversations central to Christian preaching, they are only one of the sets of voices in play. The preacher is no mere megaphone, the listener is no mere fan. If the energy of the Scriptures is to be taken seriously, those other voices need to have a say in the back and forth. The Word of God is an interactive word; to be effective in a sermon, it needs to sound forth as such. All the participants' voices need to be played—not as a deadly panel discussion (don't you just hate sitting through those?), not as a raucous verbal free-for-all, but like the unfolding moves in

an absorbing game—voice answering voice, affirming, contradict-
ing, challenging, and evoking.

Sermon research involves listening with senses on total alert for
the energy that both generates and is generated in interchange. Listening for gaps and awkward silences. Listening for sounds of people
talking all at once, even trying to shut one another down. In preparing sermons, I seek to shape a delineated space where voices can engage one another in a discussion in which stakes are high and all are
invested. Sermon shaping creates in the ears of listeners an energy flow

A. Find what's up in the air and pass it back and forth

B. Good preaching is playing conversational volleyball

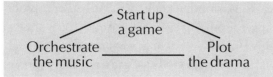

C. Good preaching is playing a rhetorical concerto	D. Good preaching is playing a theological mystery
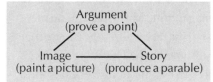	1. Clear first take
	2. Complicating tension
	3. Critical turn
	4. Culminating thrust
Integrate *all* the instruments, but *feature* only *one*	Unfold an *adventure* through *sequence* and *suspense*

Figure 4. Characteristics of effective preaching

that makes sense of the Gospel—kinesthetically moving, meeting, missing, clashing, repositioning, and reconnecting voices.

What does it feel like when your boss gathers you and your colleagues to hear the word handed down from on high? What would it feel like if, instead, your leader convened you and your colleagues to talk things through (and you actually did it!)? At the end of the day, the last words in the two gatherings might turn out to be the same; yet their forms could hardly be more different. The former would be an *ex cathedra* pronouncement; the latter would be a spirited conversation. Which would you more welcome if it were billed as "The Word of the Lord"? Which sermon sound makes more sense of the Gospel? How might we, as preachers, find our way into forms of speech that consistently and faithfully represent the Word of the One who said, "Come now and let us reason together"—and that to an irrational bunch?

Why are the Scriptures in the center of figure 4A, and where is the Holy Spirit? The Scriptures are the dynamic matrix—the sounding source from which the back and forth begins, the magnetic drawing point toward which the various interchanges converge. As for the Holy Spirit's work—that is so important it cannot be depicted as a single element. Look, then, to the arrows in the diagram and envision them as red! The dotted lines around the players indicate that each has its own integrity, but is open to sharing and receiving illuminating, interpreting words from all the others (each is a semipermeable membrane of sorts). Since the Scriptures are themselves witness to the interaction of preachers and faith communities that are in a cultic setting and a liturgical context, the voices around the edges represent an extending of God's continually creative activity of revelation—something much more powerful than a frozen-for-all-time word that must then be decked out in modern dress so as to make it seem relevant to our time and place.

A sermon that reverently, passionately plays with fire embodies the form and content of God's Revelation and plays as though in a game . . . *and* as though in a production of well-orchestrated music.

Preaching as Music

No single metaphor can convey the methods involved in the multi-faceted art of kindling a sermon. Voices need to interact with one another in the back and forth of Spirit-ed conversation, playing not only in how they interact, but also in how they sound. Think for a moment about the distinctive sounds of different musical instruments. A musical score designates a particular, distinctive melody by representing it as a series of notes spread across a staff. But that melody sounds quite different when played by a violin, a trumpet, or an oboe.

The artistic medium for a preacher is the sound of words. But words, like notes, can be played in different ways. This is literally true in the sense that physical sound production renders distinctive the voices of preachers old and young, male and female, Hispanic and African American. But I have in mind now a more metaphorical understanding of the different ways in which words can sound—differences that mark distinctive literary genres. Let me play for you the sounds of three distinguished preaching colleagues, each having a distinctive way with words. All three have a common sermon theme: the inordinate use of material possessions. (They also have a common source: the appointed readings in the Episcopal Lectionary for Proper 21 C.)

Here is a piece from preacher number one:

> *Woe to you who are complacent in Zion,*
> *and to you who feel secure on Mount Samaria.* . . .

> *You lie on beds inlaid with ivory*
> *and lounge on the finest couches.*
> *You dine on choice lambs*
> *and fatted calves.*

You strum away on your harps like David
and improvise on musical instruments.

You drink wine by the bowlful
and use the finest lotions,
but you do not grieve over the ruin of Joseph.

Therefore you will be among the first to go into exile;
your feasting and lounging will end.

(Amos 6:1–7 NIV)

Now listen to words from preacher number two:

Godliness with contentment is great gain. For we brought nothing into the world, and we can take nothing out of it; but if we have food and clothing, we will be content with that. People who want to get rich fall into temptation and a trap and into many foolish and harmful desires that plunge human beings into ruin and destruction. For the love of money is a root of all kinds of evil. Some people, eager for money, have wandered from the faith and pierced themselves with many griefs. (Verses 6–10)

Command those who are rich in this present world not to be arrogant nor to put their hope in wealth, which is so uncertain, but to put their hope in God, who richly provides us with everything for our enjoyment. Command them to do good, to be rich in good deeds, and to be generous and willing to share. In this way, they will lay up treasure for themselves as a firm foundation for the coming age, so that they may take hold of the life that is truly life. (1 Timothy 6:17–19 NIV)

Last, hear these familiar words from preacher number three:

> There was a rich man who was dressed in purple and fine linen and lived in luxury every day. At his gate was laid a beggar named Lazarus, covered with sores and longing to eat what fell from the rich man's table. Even the dogs came and licked his sores.
>
> The time came when the beggar died and angels carried him to Abraham's side. The rich man also died, and was buried. In hell, where he was in torment, he looked up and saw Abraham far away, with Lazarus by his side. So he called to him, "Father Abraham, have pity on me and send Lazarus to dip the tip of his finger in water and cool my tongue, because I am in agony in this fire."
>
> But Abraham replied: "Son, remember that in your lifetime you received good things, while Lazarus received bad things, but now he is comforted here and you are in agony. And besides all this, between us and you a great chasm has been fixed, so that those who want to go from here to you cannot, nor can anyone cross over from there to us."
>
> The rich man answered: "Then I beg you, Father, send Lazarus to my father's house, for I have five brothers. Let him warn them, so that they will not also come to this place of torment."
>
> Abraham replied, "They have Moses and the prophets; let them listen to them." "No, Father Abraham," the rich man said; "but if someone from the dead goes to them, they will repent." Abraham said to the man, "If they do not listen to Moses and the prophets, they will not be convinced even if someone rises from the dead." (Luke 16:19–31 NIV)

It would be easy to jump to the conclusion that preacher number three is the one to be emulated. But it is description, not ranking, that is the point: how does each preacher employ language to help listeners make sense of a message about possessions that is always hard to hear?

Preacher number one addresses an audience whose physical senses have been stimulated beyond satiation. Imagine him trying to engage their attention with a conceptual analysis of the moral evils of conspicuous consumption, and their failed responsibilities, as children of the covenant, to those who are starving! How well would the preacher be heard if he did? Notice, then, how his sermon unfolds. He appeals, literally, to their senses—from the sight of inlaid ivory, to the feel of fine couches, to the taste of beef and wine, to the sound of strumming instruments, to the smell of fine lotions. Having entered their awareness gently through the already open door of their comfortable consciousness, the preacher suddenly turns up the volume: "But you do not grieve over the ruin of Joseph" (in other words, there is one sense you are seriously lacking). Then he announces the implications: "Therefore you will be among the first to go into exile; your feasting and lounging will end."

Who knows how many partygoers hit the sawdust trail at the altar call of Amos? But I'll bet he got their attention! Notice how: by using picture language, the language of images. An argument is implied, surely. The sad story of a people's unfaithful response to their faithful God is in the background. But what the congregation sees and hears theologically is mediated through what it sees and hears physically. If Amos were an instrument in the orchestra, I envision him as a trumpet or a French horn. There is no mistaking the sound of his voice. It is out front—clear—not reflective or indirect. This is a poet preacher—one who makes sense of the Gospel by resorting primarily to sensory word pictures: Look! Listen! Taste! Touch! Feel!

But doesn't preacher number two use pictures as well? Well, yes, a few: "food and clothing," "trap," "root," "pierced themselves." But though his sermon is on the same topic as preacher number one's, it doesn't sound the same, partly because the proportion of explicit image-generating language is much lower. And even the images that do appear are employed in a different way. They are brief exhibits in an elaborate case set forth by the preacher. They are illustrations for listeners to reflect on, rather than immediate sensory stimuli.

Paul (the actual or implied author of this sermon) is instructing his young apprentice in how to handle a pastoral problem. His preaching imagination is fired by a desire to make sense through concept and argument. He makes a complex claim: "Beneath the apparent attractiveness of wealth, there is reason to be on guard against the sensory gratification of wealth. At the end of your life, you can't take it with you, and experience teaches that it makes false promises here and now. Wealth is a counterfeit of true riches—pursue those instead!"

The language primarily employed is the language of ideas, not images. Paul is not half the poet Amos is. Paul is (no surprise) a philosopher. Although his subject matter is roughly the same as that of his elder preaching colleague, his voice is different. If Amos sounds like a trumpet, Paul, I suggest, sounds like an oboe or a clarinet (or perhaps a bassoon!). There is a reflective, ethereal quality in his playing. His words are less direct and immediate than those employed by Amos. "You need to stop and think about the direction of your behavior! Pause! Consider!"

Whether preacher number three is Jesus himself or Jesus as portrayed through the voice of Luke is not of concern here. In the narrative of Luke's Gospel, we have just learned that the Pharisees are making fun of Jesus "because they are lovers of money." Jesus has already tried to address their self-satisfying sufficiency by depicting a manager on the take, who is suddenly forced to cut his losses when he is found out. Jesus then further analyzes the issue of inordinate possessions in terms of a relative assessment of ultimate gains and losses (in this he is not unlike preacher number two). But this strategy doesn't seem to be getting him anywhere. These followers of the Law seem convinced that they can have their cake and eat it too. They see no conflict of interest between having a hold on this world's goods, and being in good with the Law of Moses. So preacher number three begins his sermon.

At first, he sounds strikingly similar to preacher number one— vivid word pictures, detail upon detail. He doesn't sound much like preacher number two—precept upon concept, abstraction punctuated by brief evidentiary illustration. But something is different in this sermon. It uses more than word pictures to make sense of the matter of inordinate possessions. The images both shape and fit a setting. Characters of different temperaments, in different circumstances, interact with each other. Most important, the back and forth of their actions and conversations culminates at a point that, though unexpected, is reasonable in retrospect. (There are some sobering fire references in this sermon, to which we will return.)

The language here is the language of story, which has a logic not unlike that deployed by preacher number two, but in this case played out in an unfolding sequence of interpersonal encounters. The argument (as in the sermon of preacher number one) is not made explicit or proposed to the congregation for assessment. There is a "take it or leave it" quality—immediacy, yet unfolded not as a series of snapshots (as in the sermon of preacher number one), but as a swelling tide of events. This preacher makes sense by a story that connects with the ebb and flow of the day-to-day—then follows the trajectory of those events until they lead over the edge. This preacher's language tries to make sense by saying not, "Stop and look!" or "Pause and consider!" but, "Come along and see where this is leading." I think of this preacher as a viola or a cello. There is a sweep to this preacher's manner that sounds like strings.

Image, idea, story—picture, point, parable. Those ways with words are different. The differences are determined by the entire context, rather than by the individual words. (Indeed, almost any word or phrase—even most sentences or paragraphs—could find their way fittingly into any one of the three genres.)

We began this section speaking of preaching as music, and have ended up seeming to talk about literary genres instead. What's the connection? I am suggesting explicitly now (as I began to do several pages back) that preaching involves playing with language much as a musician plays with instruments in the orchestration of a composition. Flutes, violins, and trombones all make a distinctive contribution. But each gives place to the other, depending on what kind of concerto is being played.

As figures 4B and 4C suggest, good preaching not only involves playing conversational volleyball, it also involves playing a rhetorical concerto, where the objective in the orchestration is to integrate all the instruments but feature only one. Different orchestral strategies can (and should) be used to make sense of the Gospel. But not all strategies can be employed at once.

A brief illustration may show why (though it requires a shift to metaphors associated with sight). In an image sermon, the preacher stands primarily behind the congregation, so that all eyes are fixed on the images being portrayed. In a story sermon, the preacher is positioned alongside the congregation, to be in sight as a guide out of the corner of the eye. In an idea or argument sermon, the preacher (figuratively) faces the congregation, manifesting respect for the thought processes that lead to decision, rather than blindsiding the conversation partner. Shifts in viewpoint can be, even need to be, strategically engendered. But indiscriminate shifts of attention will be disorienting.

Clearly, different biblical texts tend to make sense in different ways. Different preaching occasions call for different ways of using words (to picture, to prove, or to provide parabolic movement). Different preachers have different centering strengths. And different congregations tend to listen with different kinds of ears. There are no rules for how a preacher must make sense of the Gospel. But there are strategic variables through which to exercise kindling artistry in preaching.

What is so special about the particular genres of discourse that we have described as image, idea, and story? We make sense of the world through an interplay of perception, cognition, and interaction. We could not negotiate our way through life without immediate sensations, reflective analyses, and intentional interpersonal interchanges.

Imagine how much you would know if you were denied not just one or two of your physical senses (which you occasionally have been, when you have suffered a bad cold), but all five at once? (Helen Keller could neither see nor hear, but she came alert to the meaning of the world through the sense of touch.) Imagine yourself with all antennae alert, but incapable of processing your perceptions in any reflective conceptual frame of reference. All the sensing in the world would not enable you to apprehend, let alone announce, "That makes sense!" You could not even use language unless you were able to think abstractly.

But sense making also is embedded in a communal matrix of meaning. Imagine how much good your sense-making acuity would do you had you not come to a sense of self in an environment of interpersonal activities. How much would you know if you were struck with amnesia? Why is it hard for those who have been abused to keep meaning together, regardless of how perceptive or cognitively adept they are? Why is it so hard to make a move, geographically or vocationally? Why are we undone when someone whom we have always trusted turns out to have been leading us on? In each case, there is a sense of deep disorientation, resulting not from a loss of ability to make sense through perceptions or concepts, but because the stream of events and interactions through which life has been intelligible has suddenly been interrupted.

Playing with Fire: Preaching Words as Kindling Art

	Argument
	Image ——————— Story
1. Primary "choir" of rhetorical "instruments"	Concepts, issues, claims, and critical analyses Sense impressions, feelings, moods, and gut reactions ——— Character, conflict, crisis, and conduct
2. Particular kind of sermon invitation	"Pause and consider" "Stop and look" ——————— "Come and see"
3. Literary device used to shape "grace note"	Cogent explanations Fresh associations ——— Engaging identifications
4. Underlying assumptions	Reflection fosters understanding Sight generates insight ——— Drama evokes recognition
5. Stance of preacher relative to congregation	Facing Behind ——————— Somewhere alongside
6. Point of sermon	Precisely what the sermon tries to prove Difficult to state/trivial if stated ——— Inseparable from the unfolding action
7. Similar literary genre	Expository essay Poetry ——————— Novel, play, short story
8. Similar biblical materials	Epistles, prophetic exhortations Psalms, wisdom literature, prophetic visions ——— Narrative materials in Hebrew Scriptures and Gospels
9. Similar material in teachings of Jesus	Extended discourses Short (picture) parables ——— Long (plot) parables

This pattern is drawn from our *distinct* but interconnected ways of making sense of the world:

Cognition (reflective)
Perception (immediate) ——— Interaction (intentional)

Primary sermon orientation will be informed (but not dictated) by these elements:

1. Preacher's natural voice
2. Text's fundamental shape
3. Congregation's mode of receptivity
4. Occasion's particular need
5. Message's primary thrust

Figure 5. Orchestrating the music

68

What we rely on to make sense of what we receive, we also depend on in communicating with others. We could not connect unless we assumed that others make sense as we do. In our attempts to hear God's Word, and to foster hearing in others, all we have at our disposal for evoking spiritual understanding are the media available to embodied beings. The three preachers cited in this discussion were faced with a task of making extraordinary sense by ordinary means. Their only option was to play with words in an attempt to make sense of God's Word. Their respective strategies are summarized in figure 5.

Preaching as Drama

Preaching fire is effectively kindled through the particular energies akin to play in games and in music and also (and perhaps most important) in drama.

The nouns *drama* and *play* are often used interchangeably. Drama shares something of the kinds of energy found in games and in music. All three activities unfold over time and involve cooperative participation (for example, competitors must respect the rules in order for a game to go on). However, games and music create their own forms of meaning, distinct from the events of everyday life, whereas dramas take a slice of daily living and frame it for participant observation. We see ourselves in the characters of a drama, though our circumstances differ from theirs. Skill is required to enter a role so that the player comes across as real, immersed in the tide of human affairs. What distinctively identifies drama is a plot, a narrative logic unfolding through clash and conflict, moving through suspense toward resolution.

This sounds similar to what we have just said about story as a form of playing sermon music. All stories do have plots. But plots, unfolding adventures of discovery, also operate in other places. Scientific investigations, legal cases, even picture galleries, slide shows, and multimedia events can be organized according to the logic of discovery, and are usually more effective if they are. The sequence of ideas, images, and stories constituting a sermon must be presented in the form of a plot. Sermons need to be animated by dramatic fire. The operation of grace cannot simply be exclaimed: "Amazing!" (and then, perhaps, explained, or illustrated). There is homiletical wisdom in the first verse of the hymn "Amazing Grace": "I once was lost, but now I'm found; was blind, but now I see." An effective sermon does not necessarily contain personal testimony. But it takes listeners step-by-step, scene-by-scene, insight-by-insight on a journey akin to the journey described in that line of the hymn. Why? For several reasons:

- *The givens of an oral genre.* Preaching is a performance art deployed in a temporal sequence, not a visual art or a reflective essay. A sermon comes out as a succession of sounds, rather than a fixed display of visible objects or a set of printed pages that can be turned back and revisited. A sermon keeps listeners orientated through a series of moves that shape sequences of anticipation and resolution.
- *The integrity of the listener.* Preaching is a presentation that issues open invitations, not a pronouncement that imposes directed verdicts. As preachers, we hope and pray that what we have seen and heard will evoke a spark of recognition in our listeners—that what burns within us will burn within them. But conviction is appropriately evoked through commendation, not coercion. Amazing grace forced is neither amazing nor graceful. Listeners cannot but feel pressured if confronted with sermons that sound like offers they cannot refuse. A sermon plot provides a pattern of organization that listeners can choose to follow—or not.
- *The participation of the speaker.* Preaching is an engagement that offers guided tours and shared experiences, not an announcement of assigned lessons and graded exercises. Effective sermons teach their listeners by leading them out or through. In typical schoolroom in-

struction, teachers impart and dispense. They have already grasped what the students are to grasp (and be graded on). In preaching, all are participant pilgrims. A plotted sermon is not just a spoonful of sugar that makes the (instructional) medicine go down; it re-presents a journey the preacher has already taken and also takes again with the congregation.

- *The character of contemporary culture.* Our society is a pluralistic, option-demanding association of individuals, not a single community uncritically accepting common authority. While people are manipulated by subtle conditioning forces, for such forces to be effective, they must at least appear to be chosen. Personal authenticity is a canon that cannot be violated in the ears of most of our contemporaries. Sermons that play as dramas, without manipulating, exercise appropriate influence among those who yearn to find out for themselves.

- *The nature of a spiritual faith journey.* The life to which the Scriptures invite us is an exploratory pilgrimage, not a course in skill mastery. The life of faith is not a task to be accomplished through a series of steps that can be checked off. "Been there, done that" is the testimony of someone who hasn't a clue of what faith is about. Since plots play out journeys of continually deepening discovery, they are a media well suited for embodying the Christian message.

- *The historical-eschatological trajectory of God's creating-redeeming acts.* The Gospel proclaimed in preaching is an unfolding mystery, not a fixed intelligibility. The Good News is an announcement of God's mighty acts, begun, continuing, and moving toward full expression. The stories we find in the Scriptures are not illustrations of Gospel Truth. They are manifestations, outworkings, enactments of it. If God is on the move, so must preaching be.

If all this is so, it is possible to name qualities of sermons that appropriately play with fire by plotting the drama of amazing grace:

71

- *Spark*. An immediately established, continually maintained point of contact, a piquing place of interest and identification with the drama of human life
- *Specificity*. A constant recourse to particular persons, places, objects, and feelings, not just (or primarily) abstractions, concepts, universals, and ideals
- *Significance*. An exploratory venture into matters in which something is at stake for those who listen
- *Stress*. An honest, appropriately vivid depiction of what is complex, confusing, and conflicted in the issues and concerns that are at stake
- *Sequence*. An unfolding of the story's elements in a narrative logic, a playing out of images, events, ideas, and actions over well-defined and well-directed dramatic time, a movement from and to
- *Suspense*. A deliberate, strategic delay in the introduction of that toward which the dramatic-divine action has been leading; an appropriately shaped space for dramatic complication and crisis
- *Surprise*. An infusion of critical turn, and of climax—where the nod of observation and the lure of anticipation transpose into the shock of recognition, where the utterly unexpected becomes redemptively apparent
- *Satisfaction*. A realistic resolution or reformulation of the complex issues that generates not closure but open spiritual direction
- *Spacing*. An appropriate pacing and proportion in the unfolding of the story's elements to achieve coherence among them all

This list can sound abstract, so let us supplement it with metaphorical descriptions of sermons organized in ways that almost always misrepresent the dynamic play of Holy Fire at work in amazing grace:

- *Grocery list*. Listing one idea after another, though all the ideas may come from a single section of the theological supermarket
- *Rabbit trail*. Racing, with high energy, from one high point to the

next, scampering every which way across the theological landscape
- *Forest wandering.* Meandering meditatively from place to place, stopping here or there to observe and reflect on what is in view
- *Airplane holding pattern.* Circling the same terrain over and over
- *Meeting minutes.* Moving by bullet points, recording proceedings in order, abstracted from the energy of conversational interchanges
- *Essay headings.* Setting forth evidence according to the canons for the composition of expository prose
- *Travel brochure.* Summarizing what one might encounter by signing on for the adventure as opposed to actually undertaking the journey
- *Personal diary.* Recounting in detail the preacher's own process of searching for a sermon

This set of tongue-in-cheek strategies suggests how many ways sermons, even well-planned ones, can go awry by failing to plot. (And in my time I have preached them all, which is why I can name them so easily.) There is something of value in each, obviously; but just as obviously, such organizational strategies almost never lead listeners on journeys of spiritual discovery.

How can a preacher, immersed in the preparation, know when the sermon is "plotting" and when it isn't? There are no infallible rules, yet there are indicators. We can survey the sequence of sections in the sermon (paragraphs, main moves, and so on), then experiment with it by trying to (1) rearrange the order of sections, (2) eliminate sections, or (3) add sections, or some combination of those options. (We don't want to rewrite the whole sermon! We just want to play lightly with alternatives.) When we are done, we can ask, "What does the sequence now feel and sound like?"

- If the sermon thus experimentally reshaped sounds just as clear and engaging as it did before, that is a bad sign! (That means the sermon is going nowhere in particular; there is no integral dynamic movement in the plot structure.)

73

- If the sermon thus reshaped sounds less clear, that is a good sign. (It means that the plot emerging in the preparation process has narrative structure—a logic of adventure plotting the drama of amazing grace—and, since it isn't broken, it shouldn't be fixed.)

There is another way to check for emerging plot sense: At each major juncture in the sermon text or outline, we can stop and ask, "How did we get here?" and "Where do we go from here?" Then, surveying the whole, we can ask these questions:

- "As I come to the end, do I have a sense of: 'Now I see! This makes sense!'"
- "What specific, previous steps have helped me to anticipate and discover this without announcing or explaining it in advance?"
- "What is extraneous to the sense of movement (and would best be taken out—in spite of how splendid it is in itself—because it may be literally misleading)?"
- "What is implicit but not articulated, without which listeners may be left hanging?"

Asking those questions on behalf of our listeners may make the difference in whether they will be able to play too, in whether the fire we see will be fire they can follow.

As illustrated in figure 4D, what we are attempting in this drama of sermon play is an unfolding adventure through sequence and suspense (suspending the experience of the Good News until listeners come to a sense of what's good in the news, and why it is good).

Rather than announcing that God delivered the children of Israel through the Red Sea (which we already know) and God will do something similar for us in our circumstances (which is an abstract reassurance), a plotted sermon leads listeners on a journey of deliverance, enabling them to encounter the pillar of fire for themselves.

Game, Music, Drama: Playing the Pieces Together

We have now considered play as a way of envisioning the work of stage 2 preparation. The metaphorical methodology of game, music, and drama, I think, indicates what we are doing, as we invest energy in the plunging-in phase. The more we work with these play strategies, the more we will be able to work through them. They will, at the unconscious level of habit, inform our preaching preparation. We will listen for interactivity (game), genre sound quality (music), and unfolding adventure (drama) throughout the demanding process of exegesis and interpretation. At various points in the process, we may lose the sense of where we are going. But reminding ourselves of what we are about can re-center our energy.

But what does that sound and feel like? Let's return to preacher number three—the voice of Jesus as presented by Luke. In chapter 3, we described Luke's preaching voice as involving the questions "How is healing heard?" and "How is hearing healed?" As he comes to the end of his witness to God's healing Word, Luke turns his attention to the Resurrection. He doesn't show Jesus bursting forth from the tomb. He does allow us to overhear and observe the encounter of disciples with the risen Christ. But we will miss much of what Luke has to share with us, as fellow preachers, if we take the Emmaus road account as simply Luke's affirmation that Jesus rose from the dead. Let us look at this Resurrection appearance through the eyes and ears of a kindling artist—a preacher charged with the task of playing with fire. First, the text:

> Now on that same day two of them were going to a village called Emmaus, about seven miles from Jerusalem, and talking with each other about all these things that had happened. While they were talking and discussing, Jesus himself came near and went with them, but their eyes were kept from recognizing him. And he said to them, "What are you discussing

with each other while you walk along?" They stood still, looking sad. Then one of them, whose name was Cleopas, answered him, "Are you the only stranger in Jerusalem who does not know the things that have taken place there in these days?" He asked them, "What things?" They replied, "The things about Jesus of Nazareth, who was a prophet mighty in deed and word before God and all the people, and how our chief priests and leaders handed him over to be condemned to death and crucified him. But we had hoped that he was the one to redeem Israel. Yes, and besides all this, it is now the third day since these things took place. Moreover, some women of our group astounded us. They were at the tomb early this morning, and when they did not find his body there, they came back and told us that they had indeed seen a vision of angels who said that he was alive. Some of those who were with us went to the tomb and found it just as the women had said; but they did not see him." Then he said to them, "Oh, how foolish you are, and how slow of heart to believe all that the prophets have declared! Was it not necessary that the Messiah should suffer these things and then enter into his glory?" Then beginning with Moses and all the prophets, he interpreted to them the things about himself in all the scriptures.

As they came near the village to which they were going, he walked ahead as if he were going on. But they urged him strongly, saying, "Stay with us, because it is almost evening and the day is now nearly over." So he went in to stay with them. When he was at the table with them, he took bread, blessed and broke it, and gave it to them. Then their eyes were opened, and they recognized him; and he vanished from their sight. They said to each other, "Were not our hearts burning within us while he was talking to us on the road, while he was opening the scriptures to us?" That same hour they got up and returned to Jerusalem; and they found the eleven and their companions gathered together. They were saying, "The Lord has risen indeed, and he has appeared to Simon!" Then they told what had happened on the road, and how he had been made known to them in the breaking of the bread. (Luke 24:13–35)

The gist is easy to summarize: The risen Christ appears to disciples headed for Emmaus. They don't recognize him. After an initial exchange in which they express sadness and confusion, Jesus sets them straight regarding biblical theology. When they arrive at Emmaus, the disciples invite Jesus in. Jesus breaks bread, which triggers their recognition. Jesus vanishes; the disciples return to Jerusalem. There they find others who have had analogous experiences, and they trade stories.

What happens, though, if we take it slowly, scene by scene, from the top, plotting the moves along with preacher Luke?

1. Two disciples are heading to Emmaus—talking themselves to death. Where has the Resurrection happened? In Jerusalem. Where are the tattered remnants of the Jesus community still huddled? Jerusalem. Where is the symbolic center of God's saving activity? Jerusalem. Where are these disciples going? Toward Emmaus! Do you blame them? I don't! There are many reasons why, on a day like this, one would choose to head in their direction. Yet, tragically, with respect to geography—physical and spiritual—they are heading in the wrong direction.

2. Jesus (to them a stranger) joins them—walking in the same direction! What a strange way to start a Resurrection ministry! If I were Jesus, I'd just jump out and reveal myself! Instead, he walks along with the disciples in the wrong direction!

3. Using simple words, the stranger creates a nonintrusive open space in which the disciples can begin to reflect on where they are going. "What are you talking about?"—"How could you not know? Everyone knows the things that have gone on!"—"What things?" Without telling them how limited their frame of reference is, he suggests that the lens they are employing may not be adequate for interpreting their experience. Is the stranger's move successful? Well, it does break the momentum of their walking and talking, for, in response to his questions, "they stood still, looking sad."

4. Given a spacious hearing, the disciples recount for the stranger a narrative of disintegration, despair, and disorientation. Since the stranger invites it, the tale of hope and horror spills out—early success, high expectations, cruel execution, unsettling reports, seemingly contradictory evidence. The disciples do not misrepresent a single detail. They speak the truth as far as they know it, and nothing but the truth as they understand it. They just have not, thus far, been able to hear or to see the whole truth.

5. The stranger, after hearing them out, offers a second, more challenging invitation to reflect on the direction in which they are going. "Oh, foolish ones!" he begins. That could be read with a condemning tone. There are no directions in Luke's script forbidding such a tone. Yet to use it would be inconsistent with the compassionate strategy of open invitation the stranger has employed thus far. If the stranger has not chosen, Superman style, to reveal himself in an accosting flash, why would he issue a sudden put-down after they have done nothing but answer the question that he has asked? The disciples need to be set free from their limited vision. It doesn't follow that the stranger begins the task of freeing them by setting them up.

But he does say, "Oh, how foolish you are, and slow of heart to believe." What could that mean? Have you ever encountered a puppy tangled up in his own leash? Have you ever come upon a child who can't go anywhere because she has tied her laces to shoes on opposite feet? Your heart goes out spontaneously. Stifling an outburst of laughter (you don't mean to shame them, after all), you say, with sympathy: "Silly boy! Silly girl!" Then you proceed to help untangle them

78

from the knots they have worked themselves into. Have you read the classic tales of Winnie-the-Pooh, by A. A. Milne? When Pooh Bear gets himself caught in a tight spot (as when he eats so much honey that he gets wedged in Rabbit's hole), the gentle response of Christopher Robin is, "Silly Old Bear!"

It is hard for me to envision the stranger being less compassionate. True compassion involves not just patient sympathy but redemptive reeducation. These disciples are to be pitied, but they are still stuck! "Was it not necessary for the Messiah to suffer these things?" the stranger continues. Note his next move: he again raises the possibility, first noted in scene 3, that there might be another way to make sense out of the senselessness they are suffering.

6. The stranger gracefully supplements the previously poured-out narrative of disintegration, despair, and disorientation with a narrative of reorientation, reconstitution, and re-creation. Luke's text tells us that "beginning with Moses and all the prophets," the stranger "interpreted to them the things about himself." Schooled as we are in critical and didactic methodologies, we might assume that Jesus did a close textual analysis. But there is another alternative, one I think more likely. The stranger would have explained the Scriptures (from Moses and the prophets) by recounting a familiar, but deeply healing tale for ears so wounded, perhaps as follows:

> *We were slaves in Egypt, bound under Pharaoh's bitter yoke. We were as good as dead. But with a mighty hand, through the leading of Moses, God brought us out of Egypt, across the Red Sea, into the Land of Promise.*
>
> *Out of death, into life—that's how God deals with those God loves!*
>
> *But we did not follow God's covenant of mutual care and respect—love for God, and love for neighbor. The prophets warned us of the graves we were digging for ourselves. We did*

not listen, and into exile we were carried. We hung up our harps upon the willows. How could we sing God's song in a strange land? We were as good as dead. And yet, with a mighty hand, through the work of an unwitting servant named Cyrus, God brought us out of exile, into our own land once more.

Out of death, into life—is there a pattern to discern in the hand of God?

And now, of course, as a preacher, I am getting antsy! "Bring it on home, Jesus!" I want to shout. "You've got them right where you want them—right where they need to be. Drive home your conclusion! Now's the time to tell them exactly who you are!" Jesus, the stranger-preacher, pays me no attention. Instead . . .

7. The stranger makes a move to leave, giving the disciples even more journey space in which to make their own responses to how he has reframed the situation. In simplest terms, rather than pushing on through, Jesus pulls way back. What kind of preaching strategy is this, anyway?

8. The disciples invite the stranger to stay for supper. They now make their own move, doubtless in some respects ingrained—offering hospitality to a fellow traveler at the end of a day on the road. Yet in the open spaces of Luke's account, you can almost hear the unspoken longing: "We have to hear more! Things now seem different, but it isn't clear how! We can't just bid farewell! We have to keep talking!" So, plans for supper get under way.

9. Jesus makes a wordless move by breaking bread—triggering recognition—then disappears (giving the disciples even more space to make their next move). All it takes is breaking bread. And yet that isn't right. Bread has been broken by the Bread who was broken—the One who has been breaking bread for an entire afternoon's journey. No wonder they recognize him—it has finally all come together. (And aren't you glad, Preacher David, that

Preacher Luke—and Preacher Jesus—have been smart enough not to take your advice!) But just when it seems like it should be time to stay and celebrate, there goes Jesus, making moves that shape space again. (He seems to have a thing about that!)

10. To each other, the disciples observe, "Were not our hearts burning when he was explaining the Scriptures on the road?" Most extraordinary! They never mentioned that heart burn while they were on the road. Perhaps because Luke wanted our attention focused somewhere else, and didn't want us to get distracted with too much at once. I think, however, that on the road, they were not aware of the fire kindling within them by the One who was playing it. It was the stranger's strategic plot delay, preparing them for what they could only subsequently appreciate because they had been absorbed, step-by-step, in the interpretive journey that turned death into life.

11. The disciples return to Jerusalem. They have had a literal conversion experience. They have been turned around—not by the Resurrection of Jesus per se, but by the proclamation of that Resurrection in a way that makes sense to them, a way that heals their hearing, so that they can hear that they have been healed.

But we are getting ahead of ourselves. The journey is not over. They head toward Jerusalem in the dark. Jesus is no longer with them. The mind starts to play all sorts of tricks after dark. One thing is certain: these two disciples now find themselves in precisely the same situation as that of the women whose indirect testimony they earlier questioned (if not discounted altogether). What will they say when they get to Jerusalem?

12. Arriving in Jerusalem, they hear from other disciples that Jesus got there ahead of them. From the outside looking in, there is an element of delightful humor here. Bursting in, the Emmaus two blurt out what they regard as astounding news—only to be met by: "Oh, yeah! He's been here already!" Yet there is deep grace

81

here too. The Resurrection story is not the property of any one individual or group. What is too good to be true is confirmed in an interplaying company of witnesses.

13. The Emmaus disciples tell their own story (which does for the other witnesses what it did for them)—how Jesus was made known to them in the breaking of the bread. The nighttime run back from Emmaus to Jerusalem has not been a waste of time. The Emmaus two are not denied their opportunity to extend the preaching mission, just because Jesus has already done for the Jerusalem disciples what he has done for them. Their own experience is confirmed in the retelling (we always preach to ourselves, don't we?). And, as noted earlier, the power of the story is reinforced—a good thing, because there will be many whose self-perceived interests will not be enhanced, once word gets around.

Note the last line: the disciples from Emmaus told the disciples in Jerusalem how Jesus had been made known to them in the breaking of the bread. Yet before they had headed back to Jerusalem, they had told each other that their hearts were burning when Jesus explained the Scriptures on the road. Well, which was it? Where, exactly, did the revelation come? I think the answer is "Yes!"

What we have here, I am convinced, is not simply an account of the Resurrection, but a suggestion made by Luke, the rhetorical physician, for how the form of Resurrection preaching can and should resonate deeply with the content. How the medium can become the message. From the metaphorical vantage point we have been employing, it is illuminating to reflect on how this Resurrection sermon plays with fire. The light of new life comes alive through preaching that transmits fire by strategies of play.

The interplay of the Scriptures (Moses and the prophets), community (the devastated social location of the two disciples), liturgy (the blessing of the bread), culture (the unholy politics of powers that be in Jerusalem and Rome), and preacher (the stranger's own experience—drawn on, but not imposed) suggests that Luke has played a good game in this sermon. Back and forth go the energizing moves.

The interplay of image, story, and idea is also evident. The primary rhetorical instrument, obviously, is story—this sermon, as it happens, just is the story. And the story of death and doom as well as the stories of out of death, into life, from Moses and the prophets, all play a role within the wider, total sermon story. And yet, at critical points, reflective analysis—philosophical moves, as it were—checks the inexorable downward spiral into which the despairing disciples are descending. Not once or twice, but three times, Jesus asks them to reflect on where they are going—to stand outside, to pause and consider (which is the classic strategy of an idea sermon—such as that employed by preacher number two regarding the inordinate use of possessions). Notice, however, that the break point, the critical turn, in the plot of this Resurrection sermon, is provided by a single sharp visual image: bread blessed and broken.

The unfolding flow of plot elements, the sequence and suspense that this account employs, clearly shows that Luke knows how to play. Try performing on this sermon the first check I suggested for determining when a sermon is plotting. What would have happened if Luke had altered the sequence of the scenes? Pull any of them out, or switch any of them around, and the sermon loses its punch, possibly falls flat. Add a scene at any point, and chances are good that attention will drift. The plot works because the drama plays as it should.

Stage 2 preaching preparation is arduous; amazing grace isn't cheap. Kindling artistry is work; but playing with fire can be fun!

83

Interlude

Three Illustrations of Sermon Art

How can sermons prepared with the energy of games, music, and drama make sense of the Gospel? What experiences can they kindle among those in need of Holy Fire? Here are three expressions of kindling artistry. Each, as you will see and hear, manifests an animated interplay of distinctive voices from the Scriptures, culture, congregation, and liturgy. Each leads listeners on an unfolding adventure through strategic plotting. The first uses primarily images, the second unfolds a careful argument, the third employs a story as the centering means of sparking insight. Rather than interrupting the experience by running analytical commentary, I will only set the context within which each expression of kindling art was originally offered, reserving reflective observations until all three preachers have had their say.

"Come Out, Come Out, Wherever You Are!"
A Sermon for Easter Sunday from Colossians 3:1–4 and John 20:1–18
Joy E. Rogers

"For you have died, and your life is hidden with Christ in God. When Christ who is your life is revealed, then you also will be revealed with him in glory" (Col 3:3–4).

Death and resurrection—that pretty much says it all. The punch line, or the explanation of the joke we didn't get. It's one of those things where you really had to be there. And even then it was subtle.

85

A living, breathing human being was dead and gone. The dead part was pretty much agreed upon. A lot of people saw him die. Some who loved him witnessed his anguish, turned to each other for comfort, and mourned him deeply. A few compassionate, loyal, and probably guilt-ridden souls saw to it that he had a decent burial. The dead part is pretty straightforward.

But now it gets confusing. The living man is dead; but the dead man is gone. The possibilities for explaining the dilemma are limited. "Body snatchers!" is Mary Magdalene's best guess, and she runs for reinforcements. They confirm the verdict: "Gone! The man was dead and now is gone."

So Mary does what any sensible woman in like circumstances would do. At least she does what I would do. Her menfolk have thrown up their hands and gone home. Her mourning is frustrated; she's lost, quite literally, the focus of her grief. So she bursts into tears. Two angels and then a stranger ask a useless question: "Woman, why are you weeping?" They get, in effect, the same answer: Not because he's dead (apparently she could deal with that), but because he's gone. If the dying was senseless, dead at least was reasonable; gone is just not fair.

Maybe the gardener can help. It's times like this we really want someone with the answers, the handyperson who will fix the break, seal the leak, tidy up the mess. We really often want a gardener God, a God who will give us back our dead hopes, our lost loves, our failed enterprises, a God to make it nice, not new. A God of reason and religion, not a God of death and resurrection.

And then, in an instant, it all comes apart. Suddenly, dead-and-gone feels more like hide-and-seek. God playing games—and playing fast and loose with the rules as well. "Here I come, ready or not! Catch me if you can. Now you see me, now you don't." Is this any way to run a religion?

Definitely not. But then, the church isn't in the religion business—the business of bringing the world the bad news that God will think kindly about us only after we have gone through certain creedal, liturgical, and ethical wickets. The church is in the business of proclaiming the Gospel—the business of announcing the unsettling news that God has taken all the disasters religion was trying to remedy, and has alone set them right. "While we were yet sinners, Christ died for the ungodly." And God raised him up.

Then what are we doing here, if this is not a religious enterprise? What are we doing here on a fine spring morning, dressed in our Easter best? We're having a party, and we're playing. The party game is God's game, by God's rules, and God's already won—so we do. They are not hard rules, except for the ones concerning the wild cards. You die, you rise, just like Jesus. The game is not dead-and-gone, but hide-and-seek. And just when you think God's the one hiding, you find that God's after you, seeking and seeking and seeking, no matter how good you thought your hiding place was. Just when you think you have found a caretaker who might tidy up the loose ends of your fraying life, focus your tired grief, return you to your deadly hopes, God pops out from behind a gardener. "Oley, oley in free! Tag, you're it! Now pass it on! Go and tell!"

If you think Easter makes us home free, you're a bit late. We got to home base on Friday at the cross. Once you tag up there, you're dead. Not dead and gone; dead and risen, because Jesus is. This morning is a Resurrection party, but so was last Friday. We thought that was only the dying part, but the God game isn't ever all or nothing. It is always all.

We did a Good Friday liturgy for the children this year. For the grownups, that was pretty scary—having to say words like *dead* and *blood* in front of the children. Children, however, are pretty good at this kind of game, for they haven't yet forgotten that real play is serious business, world making business. They cried out with real conviction, "Crucify him!" as we told the terrible story—a story that can give you the creeps. And they touched the cross. And trembled,

87

trembled, trembled; so did the cross. No blood of bulls or goats to make the atoning sacrifice. A few parent types to provide a threat of judgment. But mostly wiggling bodies, a song or two about a body broken, the blood shed. And in the middle of it all, a five-year-old apostle suddenly proclaims the Resurrection.

"Ready or not," God says, "here I come." The wild card. There are other weird variations on the same theme. For this is a game where the lost are always found, losers always win, the last finish first, and the best things come in small packages, like mustard seeds and incarnations.

God has left us come clues, for our own seeking, should we care to give it a whirl, just for the fun of it. "I am the light of the world," God told us, and the new fire marks our space and gathering. Sometimes God looks, for all the world, like living water. And this morning, a baby boy will die and rise with him in those waters. And we can squeal with delight if we are splashed in the spray that washes new life into being. "Gotcha!" says God.

"I am the Bread of life, the Vine that bears fruit." And the dead and risen One will feed our hungers and quench our thirst. This Gospel game is not a religious enterprise. It's play, serious play, for it is the only real play that anyone has ever known. You die, you rise, just like Jesus. The church doesn't make the rules, we just name the game; we can't even get a patent or a copyright. You don't have to join to play it; you just have to die, and God does the rest.

It's a messy business, and inconvenient. The linens are left wadded and crumpled, full of oil marks and wine stains. Water is splashed about, and there is always a trail of breadcrumbs to be swept up. Newness isn't niceness. And any God who goes around looking like a gardener isn't predictable, respectable, or comfortable.

But it's God's game, this Resurrection hide-and-seek, and there's no way of telling where God'll turn up next or what suit God'll wear. And it's God's party, this death and Resurrection party. We get to come, not because we're religious, but because it's the only game in town that losers win, and where the lost are found, where the dead are raised. How was your invitation addressed?

Resurrection hide-and-seek. We're invited not because we're good, but because we're God's; not because we're faithful, but because we're forgiven; not because we're clever, but because we're created in God's image, and re-created in a living and dying and rising again.

It's no garden party. The gardener's a fake, a fool, a sham, a clown. God's April fool's joke on us all. The man's not dead and gone, just dead and risen for you and me. So let's play. You die, you rise, just like Jesus. "Come out, come out, wherever you are!"

"I have seen the Lord," says Mary. Alleluia! He is risen!

Taking Up the Cross in a Time of War

A Sermon in Lent, Immediately Before the U.S. Invasion of Iraq in 2003, from Mark 8:31 38

Matthew Gunter

In the year 390, Ambrose, bishop of Milan, sent a letter to one of his parishioners. Ambrose was convinced that this parishioner had committed a grievous and public sin. Ambrose told the parishioner that until he repented publicly, he was excommunicated, and would not be allowed to receive Communion. This was no ordinary church member. It was Theodosius, ruler of the Roman Empire. One of Theodosius's officials had been murdered in the Greek city of Thessalonica. The exact circumstance is unknown. Perhaps it was a tax revolt. Perhaps it was a random terrorist attack. In any event, Theodosius had done what emperors do. He had sent in the army to teach the people of Thessalonica, and the rest of the empire, a lesson. Some seven thousand people—men, women, and children—were killed, the vast majority of whom had had nothing to do with the death of the official. Ambrose was not a pacifist, but he knew that the emperor's actions needed to be condemned, even if it meant the very real possibility of his being sent to prison or killed. Emperors don't usually like to be challenged. Against all odds, Emperor Theodosius repented and publicly sought absolution from his bishop.

I've been thinking a lot about Ambrose and Theodosius lately. What would Ambrose say about the looming invasion of Iraq? Would his opinion make any difference? Christian leaders around the world and the leaders of nearly every Christian denomination in America have stated that this war does not meet the standards of a just war. The pope has declared the same. But it does not seem to matter.

Some of these leaders can perhaps be written off as religious lackeys of the left—people who would reflexively oppose any use of force by America. Not all of them, however. The current pope has never been accused of being a liberal lackey. Nor has Miroslav Volf, an evangelical theologian on the faculty of Yale. There are also others who cannot easily be written off.

Some theologians have argued that a preemptive war on Iraq is justifiable. One has to wonder, though, if the religious lackeys of the left don't have their parallel among conservatives who have never seen a war waged by their own country that they could not justify. Did Theodosius have any theologians around to reassure him that his use of force was necessary and justified for the good order of the Empire? "You can't run an empire, after all, without a little collateral damage." The just-war theory has been stretched to support every war the United States and other nations have waged. Too often, the just-war theory is merely the "excuse-war theory."

I have referred, in passing, to the pending war in recent sermons, but been hesitant to address it directly. One reason for my hesitancy is that the biblical texts have not seemed to lend themselves naturally to addressing the issue of Iraq. I do not want to do violence to the Scriptures just so that I can preach against violence. Another reason for my hesitancy is that we have all heard too many preachers use the pulpit as a platform for sermonizing about their political prejudices rather than proclaiming the Gospel. I am wary of doing the same. I have also been hesitant because I am well aware that I am no Ambrose, and you are not Theodosius. None of us here has any control over the decision to attack Iraq. And, to be honest, I have been hesitant to address the topic directly because I don't particularly like controversy. But this morning's text and the urgency of the situation lead me to wade into the thicket.

Jesus said: "If any want to become my followers, let them deny themselves and take up their cross and follow me." I want to explore with you this question: "What does it mean to take up the cross in a time of war?" There has been lots of public talk about God recently, some by the president, some by those who oppose him. But talk about God can be cheap and self-serving. I am convinced that any talk about God without the cross tends to be either insipid or dangerous. There have been many examples of both lately.

What does it mean to take up the cross in a time of war? I have said before that I am persuaded that the way of the cross means a commitment to peace. It is harder to get around the nonviolence of Jesus and his earliest followers than some want to suggest. But talk of peace must not avoid the reality of sin and death. Any talk of peace implying that if we are just nice to others they will be nice to us is not the way of the cross. It is simply naïve and insipid. Any serious talk of nonviolence must recognize that it is a call to martyrdom. My own, certainly, but more problematically, that of those I might otherwise intervene to help. Being resolutely nonviolent does not mean doing nothing, but refraining from having any blood on my hands in a world of violence, sin, and death—standing by while others bleed. That is not an easy way. Yet I am not convinced that it is not the way of the cross. There is no avoiding the hard fact that whether we commit to nonviolence or to the "judicious" use of violence, we are all stretched out between the catastrophe we have made of the world and the promise of God's good creation and of God's Reign.

I am catholic enough to recognize that the majority wisdom of the church has not regarded radical nonviolence as the only faithful posture for Christians. I take that wisdom seriously. But even then we must ask, "What does it mean to take up the cross in a time of war?" The just-war approach, as usually presented, does not ask that question seriously enough. I have serious reservations about a moral system in which the particulars of Jesus's teaching, life, and cross are essentially irrelevant. Hindus, Muslims, and agnostics could all support the classic just-war approach. What does it have to do with Jesus and the cross? If we decide that sometimes we cannot avoid participating in violence, we still have to decide whether to do so in light of the cross and of Jesus. What does the way of the cross look like, then? This way must also be understood as a way of martyrdom; but not in the sense that some are going to die in a war. That is obvious. The way of the cross involves, first and foremost, dying to ourselves and following Jesus. What might that mean? At least these things:

Taking up the cross in a time of war means getting our loyalties straight. Last summer I saw a woman wearing a T-shirt that I found very troubling and very telling. It was a white T-shirt that had JESUSAVES written across the front. I believe he does. But that was not the only message on the shirt. It actually looked more like this: JE**SUSA**VES. All the letters were blue except for those in the middle—USA—which were red. It was a telling icon of the confused syncretism of many Christians in America. Who saves? Jesus? The USA? Or are the two so entwined that we can't tell the difference? We cannot begin to discern whether war in general or this war in particular is justifiable until we can tell the difference between the way of Jesus and the way of the United States. The way of the cross means dying to, and being suspicious of, all other loyalties. If talk of just war just means it is okay for Christians to kill when their government says so, it is not the way of the cross.

Taking up the cross in a time of war means following the way of humility. It means being prepared to entertain the possibility that we are wrong. It means asking, "Why does most of the rest of the world disagree with us?" Even governments that support the United States' invasion of Iraq do so against the will of the overwhelming majority of their people. Right and wrong are not determined by majority vote. But it is arrogant to presume that everyone else is automatically wrong because they don't see it our way. If it is America's fate to be the de facto empire of the world, how we live that fate out will make a big difference. The way of the cross means we must refrain from lording it over others. We have not been doing a very good job of that lately. Because the United States has been seen as lording it over others, we have remarkably managed to lose a public relations contest with a thug and tyrant like Saddam Hussein and alienated much of the world. Humility means listening to those who disagree with us, not derisively dismissing them so that we can ignore their concerns.

We might not need U.N. approval to go to war. The just-war approach allows that any nation has the right, on its own authority, to defend itself when attacked. But Iraq has not attacked us, and it is not clear that it is able to. If we are going to war to enforce U.N. resolutions, proper authority would seem to reside in the body that passed the resolutions. What does it mean to enforce the will of others against their will? What if Egypt and Syria decide, on their own, to enforce the U.N. resolutions condemning Israeli settlements on the West Bank? I do not think we would find that to our liking. We apparently haven't run out of patience there. Humility means being careful of the precedents we set just because we can.

Taking up the cross in a time of war means recognizing our own sin. This is a Lenten theme. It is a Christian theme. Much of the world looks to America as an example, a beacon of hope, liberty, and prosperity. But the world also suspects our power and our motives. We need to deny ourselves the indulgence of self-justification and recognize that their doubt is neither accidental nor simply a colossal misunderstanding. There are reasons many in the world do not trust us. I am very concerned that as a result of this war and our behavior leading up to it, we will be living with the deep resentment of much of the rest of the world for a long time. And we will be less safe and secure because of that resentment. Recognizing our sin means we need to be suspicious of our own motives. Can it be that every country that opposes war with Iraq has mixed motives, but the United States does not? Do we really believe that we are the only ones who are realistic about the dangers of the world? Do we really believe that we are the only ones who have courage? We need to take the reality and pervasiveness of sin more seriously than that.

Taking up the cross in a time of war means repenting. We need to be prepared to repent of sins we commit as individuals and as a nation. And if sometimes we decide we must resort to violence, we need to repent for that violence. Some suggest that the classic just-war approach does not presume that violence is wrong. I do not know if that is so. If it is, the just-war theory needs to be rethought in light of Jesus and the cross. Killing some people for the sake of other people is always a devil's bargain—even if we decide it is the only bargain we can make. St. Basil of Caesarea, a contemporary of Ambrose's, said that though the church may decide that we must sometimes resort to war, when we do so, we should repent. And those who participate should do penance, enduring a time of exclusion from the Sacrament. That is still the position of the Eastern Orthodox Church, which is not pacifist, but has never accepted that war can be just or pleasing to God.

Lent is about taking up the cross, denying ourselves, and following Jesus. It includes denying our tendency toward self-justification—as individuals, as a church, and as a nation. It means dying to other loyalties. It means humility. It means acknowledging our own sinfulness. It means repentance. It is a way of martyrdom. Jesus said, "If any want to become my followers, let them deny themselves and take up their cross and follow me." I can't say whether, if he were here, Ambrose would oppose war with Iraq. What disturbs me is that for many Christians in America, it wouldn't matter if he did.

People Is People

A Sermon on Mother's Day (in the Season of Easter) from John 13:34–36

Elizabeth M. Kaeton

From Episcopal pulpits around the country this morning, priests are either ignoring this day completely, or piously lecturing how the church does not celebrate secular holidays like Mother's Day or Father's Day. Yet we have hymns and prayers for national holidays in our hymnal and prayer book. And we remember saints whose lives were very secular. Such lectures, therefore, cannot be the whole truth.

Truth be told, for some of us, Mother's Day—like Father's Day—is filled with more than a measure of discomfort. For some of us, it is the pain of having lost our mothers to death. For others, it's the pain of having our mothers still alive but part of a relationship that is, if not painful, less than satisfactory. Some of us are sitting here filled with dread about this afternoon's visit or tonight's dinner. For many of us, it's about being a mother with a less-than-satisfactory relationship with our own children. Many of us live with the regret of never having had children. Or of having lost a child. Or the lingering pain and shame of long ago giving up a child for adoption—or sacrificing a child to abortion. Others of us may have never been biological mothers, but have deep, satisfying relationships with children who might just as well be our own. Others of us may know women—or men—who are more like mothers than our own biological mothers could ever be.

None of us are exempt from the messy complications of family relationships. It becomes clear, suddenly, why it might be much easier to put matters of church before matters of family. There is a comforting kind of salve that comes from imposing the rules of the church on the breaks and pains of one's heart! Into all the complications of modern life, the ancient words of Jesus come rushing like a cool wind on a hot day: "A new commandment I give to you, that you love one another; even as I have loved you, that you also love one another. By this all will know that you are my disciples, if you have love for one another" (Jn 13: 34-35).

Mind you, Jesus says all these things immediately after Judas betrays him with a kiss. He tells the Apostles these things, then bids them farewell before he is brought to trial, condemned, and crucified. What a remarkable man! No wonder he was the Son of God. No human could ever live up to the standards he met. Could they?

Let me tell you about a man who became father and mother in God to me. His name was Father Koumaranian. He was an Armenian Orthodox priest. I was newly ordained and absolutely full of beans in my new position as chaplain at the University of Massachusetts Lowell. The Armenian Orthodox Church does not ordain women, but Father Koumaranian was, apparently, enchanted with me. He had decided that, since I seemed to have some pastoral skills, and to know a little Hebrew and Greek as well as having a fair comprehension of the Scriptures, I might actually be redeemable as a priest. He was determined that if I was going to preside at divine liturgy, by God, I was going to learn to do it the right way—the ORTHODOX way. It started slowly. He would call me up on a Wednesday and say: "Mother, this is Father. We are having wedding on Saturday. It would be good for you to learn liturgy. It would be good for my people to see woman priest. You come." It was more a command than an invitation. I went. Of course, I went. It was wonderful! The incense! The chanting! The strange incantations! I loved it!

One day, he called me up and said, "Mother, this is Father. We are having funeral tomorrow. It would be good for you to learn liturgy. It would be good for my people to see woman priest. You come."

The funeral service was filled with the same mystery and

96

grandeur that marked every liturgy—Sunday Eucharist, weddings, or baptisms. The only thing changed was the makeup of the congregation. This assembly was filled with men dressed in somber black coats and row upon row of women dressed from head to toe in black—complete with black scarves tied securely under their ample chins.

It came time for the eulogy. I assumed Father would talk to the congregation in Armenian, so I was a bit taken aback to hear him begin to speak in English. "There are people in this world," he said, "who are always making you happy. They are always having a smile, or a kind word to say. They are always doing a nice thing. Just to see them on the street makes your heart bursts into song, so happy do they make you to see them." He walked over to the casket and put his hand lovingly on the top and said, "This . . . is not one of those people."

I was stunned! All I could think of was: "Please! Don't let anyone be able to read what my face is saying." My next thought was, "What the heck is he doing?" I opened my eyes and looked over at the first row of women, where the dead man's wife sat. The entire row were nodding their heads in agreement.

Then, I heard Father say: "But isn't our God so good; isn't our God so forgiving, that now, even now, this man is resting in eternal light in the loving arms of God, beloved of our Savior, Jesus Christ, and blessed by the warmth of the Holy Spirit. Because," he added, "people is people, and God is God."

In that one moment, Father Koumaranian taught me more about the love of God in Christ than had any one of my fancy-schmancy courses in seminary: "People is people, and God is God." So, stop putting such high and divine expectations on each other, and love one another as God loves us.

It's so easy to miss the point that if there's a Christ in me and a Christ in you, then there's a bumbling, stumbling, saying-all-the-wrong-things Peter in me and a bumbling, stumbling, saying-all-the-wrong-things Peter in you. And there's a doubting Thomas in me and a doubting Thomas in you. And there's a scrupulous, tax-collecting, putting-details-before-people Matthew in me, and a scrupulous, tax-collecting, putting-details-before-people Matthew in you. And there's a betraying Judas in both of us.

God is God, and people is people. We all make messes in our lives, of our lives, and in other people's lives. We don't mean to, but there it is. We hurt the very people we love, and betray our best intentions to do otherwise. The more we detest our own imperfections, the more we seem to demand perfection from others. What we fear most in ourselves, we hate most in others. Into these dilemmas, Father Koumaranian says, "People is people, and God is God."

So, if you are worried about your Mother's Day celebration—for whatever reason—or about the fact that the church's denial of reality won't make it any better, relax. God doesn't expect the same perfection you—or this culture—expect of yourself or others. Because God was in Christ, God knows our humanness—even better than we do. God knows our limitations as well as our possibilities. And God still loves us very, very much.

Just remember this: Into these modern times come the ancient words of Jesus: "A new commandment I give to you, that you love one another; even as I have loved you, that you also love one another. By this all will know that you are my disciples, if you have love for one another."

In some respects, these sermons could hardly be more different. While there are obvious differences of text and occasion, the deepest differences have to do with ways of helping listeners to make sense of the Gospel. Joy Rogers employs wave upon wave of hide-and-seek images to evoke the energy of Easter. The descriptions are visual and auditory, of course; but their primary impact is kinesthetic. Rogers re-creates the breathless sense of Resurrection shock. Matthew Gunter is, of necessity, much more measured in pace and reflective in tone. While he does set forth a systematic case against idolatrous God-and-country associations, he is concerned more with shaping a discerning space for Christian community reflection than with proving a point or winning a debate. Elizabeth Kaeton undertakes a mission into the sharp and conflicted feeling territory of complex family dynamics. Through the story of her encounter with an Orthodox priest, she gives us a place to find healing without resorting to invasive surgery.

And yet, story line and concept movement are implicit (and supportive) in Rogers's dance of images. While Gunter's language is much less immediate and vivid than Rogers's, the immediate prewar context is constantly alluded to (the preacher need not try to compete with the media!) and the story of salvation as centered in the cross is never far from consciousness. Kaeton's use of images is shaped to maximize the impact of her story. And the story itself is bounded on both ends with context setting, and with conclusion-inviting conceptual analysis.

For all their differences, however, these three preachers have much in common. All are faithful not just to the words and phrases of their biblical texts, but to the dramatic trajectories of those writings. The God on the move portrayed in each Scripture passage is dynamically re-presented in each sermon. The distinctive voices of preachers, communities, liturgical occasions, and prevailing cultural issues go back and forth throughout the sermons. Whether in strategic sequential deployment of images (Rogers), or step-by-step movement through consideration of alternatives and implications (Gunter), or development of a sermon plot in which the story plot, per se, is necessary but not sufficient (Kaeton), all three preachers convey to their listeners the transforming power of Gospel drama.

The effect on listeners, in each case, is not that of being informed, explained to, exhorted, accused, or upbraided, but that of being engaged—invited, for themselves, into the play of fire.

6

Like a Refiner's Fire

Who can endure the day of his coming, and who can stand when he appears?
For he is like a refiner's fire . . . and he will purify the descendants
of Levi and refine them like gold and silver, until they present offerings to
the Lord in righteousness. (Malachi 3:2–3)

There is more to kindling a fire than finding a spark and feeding it with care. Well-established fires need to be stirred: logs repositioned, coals raked together, ashes knocked loose. The pyre is jostled, poked at, played with to foster maximum color, light, and warmth. The analogy with preaching preparation is not precise here; all metaphors have limitations. After you get the fire going, literal tending of it is a matter of maintenance; third-stage preaching preparation moves a creative listening process forward to a place where it can foster creative hearing in others.

Perhaps we can shift the metaphoric angle slightly— from what is done to refuel a fire, to what a refining fire does: a refining fire burns away impurities in metals, anneals distinctive traits of alloys. That is what we are about in the polishing, pruning, finishing-touch play that we employ when moving from the plunging-in play of stage 2 preparation into the final stage of sermon process.

Some preachers enter stage 3, polishing play, too early. They tinker with words and phrases from the outset of their preparation.

A splendid distraction, that, from the real need of the moment, which is either to seek initial insight with soft focus, or to plunge deeply into exegetical, hermeneutical, and homiletical issues of sermon research and design with sharp focus. Yet it is also the case that many preachers do little if any stage 3 preaching play when the time for it arrives. They have had an initial "Aha!" Recognizing that the spark must be tended, they have plunged in and worked with their insights and instincts. Sometimes their initial energy has to be not just fed, but refocused; sometimes the spark just dies, necessitating a fresh start. But if the spark catches, and flame develops, if game, music, and drama strategies are carefully orchestrated through the interplay of research and design, the preacher, coming toward a sermon's conclusion, may well exult: "Aha! Got it! I'll look it over before I give it; but this is done!"

That reaction seems reasonable. Why shouldn't preachers take a rest from their labors when they've earned it? Chances are there's little time left before delivery anyway. Besides (as we discover to our unpleasant surprise), it is possible to overprepare, to keep stirring and poking so much that the fire dissipates. Yet the sermon is best served if we take a clean break after stage 2 (as we should after stage 1), and return to reengage the sermon afresh with a different focus—neither the soft focus of stage 1, nor the sharp focus of stage 2, but a synthesizing, synergizing focus.

The fact is, if we really got into research and design as we should have, we cannot help but having lost perspective. We were so long in the middle, we are now too close. Our effort to craft a sermon was a journey of preparation for us, and that journey itself may make it difficult to sense how effective the journey of listening will be for those who hear the sermon. What may have happened during the first two stages that we might need to revisit and engage at stage 3?

• What got us off and running as we began our preparation may not be the most efficient means for gaining initial attention from our listeners. (Their imaginations might be distracted by the very thing that attracted ours.)

- In the extended, intermittent process of thinking things through, we may have shifted the trajectory of the sermon plot without realizing it (since the shift was a part of the process itself). The sermon is now going someplace other than where we thought it would go when we started (or at least is proceeding to its destination by an altered route).

- Certain ideas or images may have sung so loudly in our heads as we were reading, thinking, sketching, and writing that they are obvious to us. We may all but swear that we have stated these explicitly, yet left large gaps, or made disorienting turns, for our listeners.

- We may have been so concerned about being perfectly clear that we have illustrated a point out of all proportion to its importance, or said many times over what we wanted to make sure that listeners (or, more likely, we!) would not forget.

- We may have told a story (important though it is) in greater detail than is warranted in the overall plot, and the interest levels of those who listen will therefore sag—either as we recount it or when we move on.

- We may have been so concerned about making sure listeners get the point that we left no space for awareness to dawn within them. (Preachers have a besetting tendency to perform the sermonic equivalent of explaining the joke, instead of shaping spaces within which listeners can make discoveries for themselves.)

- We may have shaped the sermon plot in a sequence that is less than fully strategic for the sermon's purpose. The flow (which may have occurred to us intuitively) may be confusing, pedantic, repetitive, or disjointed (when it plays out to listeners).

Those and other elements may need polishing. It is important to realize that those concerns in sermon drafts are not mistakes (akin to wrong answers on a math problem or a multiple-choice test). No, we have, in fact, been playing properly in the earlier stages. It is only because of those prior efforts that we are now in a position to make finishing moves that will bring the sermon fire to maximum strength. The time we devote to stage 3 may well be minimal (5–15 percent of the time expended in total preparation), but this additional investment will make a significant difference in how the sermon impacts our hearers and is retained by them. When we play with our message just a bit more in stage 3, we are not necessarily scratching an obsessive itch for perfection, or trying simply to sweeten what we have to say so that hearers will be more willing to swallow it. Rather, we are trying to make the illumination inherent in what we have prepared maximally accessible to the listening imagination. What has made sense of the Gospel to us in the context of research and reflection over time, must be presented with the greatest chance of making sense to those who will be listening in a single sitting.

This final preparation is necessary work for preachers who have labored long and hard already. But there is another dimension: stage 3 preparation is fun! All that we have worked to pull together now comes together—often in ways that surprise us (when we thought we had made our discoveries already). Images and phrases take on vitality, the sense of plot becomes both leaner and richer. The sermon finally begins to sound like itself. That may sound odd; but sermons have a life of their own. Artists in other media report a similar phenomenon—a reminder that they are not masters of their art forms, but servants of them. (A distinguished painter once told me she must listen to paints "speaking back to me, telling me in no uncertain terms how I may or may not proceed.")

The experience of being told what to say is signaled by bursts of insight through the first two stages; what is most often heard early on comes in bits and pieces, fading in and out. Now, however, we have

104

sufficient distance from what we have been doing to meet it on its own terms—and let it tell us where and how to finish. It is in this last strange kind of inspiration that you can deeply taste the joy of stage 3 preaching preparation. Stage 3 involves not trying to fix the sermon just like you want it, but rather positioning yourself to hear with greater clarity what you have been listening for all along, as you focus attention on how all related elements can be made present to listeners when the sermon comes forth live.

Some of my most fruitful, freeing times of prayer spring up spontaneously in the middle of this synergizing stage, when all the dimensions of the sermon begin to complement and resonate, and unanticipated levels of meaning cascade into consciousness. The work I do in the first two stages is my gift to God. What often happens in the pruning, polishing, fine-tuning stage is something I experience as God's gift to me.

Giving Voice to a Living Word

How do we know where and how to look and listen in this synergizing stage of preaching play? What strategic steps can we take to prune, polish, and fine-tune? No exhaustive checklist of rules can be set forth. There are, however, things to look out for and listen up for, that tend to recur from sermon to sermon and preacher to preacher. These have to do with the elements integral to an oral art form, with dynamics inherent in the Gospel (which involve the mighty acts of God that transform us over time), and with the ethics of communication (which require that we honor the personal space of our listeners, even as we commend God's Word to them). Let me offer some succinct suggestions along with a concise rationale.

Whether a sermon takes the primary shape of an image, story, or argument, it needs to draw listeners directly into the impressions, interactions, or issues it presents. An effective sermon takes us on a spiritual adventure; it does not just report what the preacher thinks, feels, or believes—and exhort listeners to think, feel, or believe the same.

That may sound obvious (after all, few of us are helped when we are subjected to lectures or harangues). But it is not easy to use words in ways that engage, convince, and inspire people without coercing, seducing, or manipulating then. Unlike most theological writings, sermons are not reports or essays.

The Gospel too is not a report or a well-crafted theme. It is an ongoing activity of divine initiative and human response, an activity that has a history, a present movement, and a specific future direction. If a sermon is a freeze-dried report of God's saving work, then the medium is not faithful to the message. As preachers, we are not in the business of reporting truths; we are in the business of attempting, in the power of the Spirit, to regenerate and extend the impact of God's mighty acts. Preaching is not primarily a propositional analysis of the conceptual implication of the ontological dimensions of divine essence; it is an adventure into the mysterious moves of God's relentless love.

If our sermons have the objectivity appropriate for reports and essays, our listeners will sense, if only half-consciously, that preacher and listener are objectively detached from each other—and that God is detached from both. An objective proclamation about how God loves us personally will actually foster the impression that God is a distant object, not a tangible presence.

How, then, can we shape our sermons to draw listeners in rather than leaving them looking on? How can preaching enable listeners to participate—but leave them free to make their own responsible decisions?

1. Give priority to these elements in your writing:

- Present tense over past tense verbs
- Active voice over passive voice
- Simple sentences over complex sentences
- Shorter sentences over longer sentences

106

Past tense, passive voice, and complex, long sentences are not always inappropriate. But those constructions convey a sense of distance. The cumulative effect of their continued use is an impression that God is there and then, rather than here and now. If past tense, passive voice, and complex sentences are used, there should be good reasons. Longer sentences may be employed to provide the variety that good writing requires. However, piling on long sentence after long sentence leaves listeners feeling like they are chasing a train as it is pulling out of the station.

2. Use concrete details and particular instances, rather than abstract generalizations. This does not mean that you should avoid concepts altogether, or multiply images indiscriminately. (Concepts can be particular; images can be abstract.) It does mean that the vaguely general is always perceived as remote. What is true universally is always best grasped by a "for instance." What is true universally is never generic; it is experienced and expressed uniquely and afresh in each special case. If we clearly depict a real person in live action, those who listen will make the leap and grasp the essence of what is true about personhood, and make the connection with their own experience.

3. Do not refer to the framework of the sermon. That is, unless there is a compelling reason for doing so, do not refer or direct attention to these elements:

- The sermon itself
- Yourself as the preacher
- Your listeners as listeners
- The Scripture texts as readings, lessons, or texts
- The liturgical texts as pieces of liturgy

Referring to the sermon's framework focuses attention on the act of preaching, listening, worshiping, or thinking about the Scriptures, rather than engaging the preacher and listeners as participants in the sermon event. Framework elements invite listeners to stand outside the sermon event and watch it from a distance—instead of entering into the journey of transformation upon which the sermon needs to take them.

To talk about a story in a story, for example, almost always undoes the impact of the story. The image on a TV screen, within a TV screen, within a TV screen . . . is framed and perceived as remote and unreal—regardless of how large a screen the viewer is actually watching. There is an important place for reflection in sermons. But the preacher must take the listeners into a reflective adventure—one that is live and immediate.

4. If possible, use direct dialogue, rather than summarizing statements about conversations, speeches, or letters. Incorporating direct dialogue invites listeners into the center of the action, rather than leaving them at the periphery. The Scriptures can often be effectively employed as direct dialogue (for example, you could say, "'Do not be conformed to this world,' Paul tells us, 'but be transformed by the renewing of your mind'"). Brief liturgical or scriptural phrases can often be incorporated into the flow of the sermon. Referring to them, however, tends to stop the action, and makes us turn and objectively observe the reference.

5. Show listeners directly, don't just tell them about it. Immerse listeners in the action of the scene or the story, or in the tension and thrust of the argument. Don't report the results or announce the conclusions. Produce scenes; don't hand out scripts sprinkled with stage directions.

6. Don't steal your own thunder by announcing where the argument, story, or image is going, before it gets there. This is the opposite of how we were taught to write essays; but it is essential when writing for the ear rather than for the eye. By careful shaping, you can prepare listeners for where you are headed—giving anticipatory intimations, and sign posts along the way. But don't give away the plot. If you do, listeners will have no incentive to follow you on the sermon's journey.

Even if your sermon is a rigorous argument, the point of which, for some compelling reason, needs to be stated first, you can still create a sense of drama and movement. For example, you could ask, "How in the world could anyone arrive at a conclusion like that?" and then take the congregation on an engaging detective hunt, maintaining dramatic tension as the train of thought unfolds.

7. In creating dramatic scenes, go to the center of the action first, then fill in background features as they become necessary for developing the plot. Do not spend time describing streams of consciousness going through the minds of story characters. Instead, describe the way those mental states register in the characters' behavior. Let listeners infer what is going on inside the characters—as they do in real life. Show them what they would see if they were in the scene; don't take them into a mental hall of mirrors.

Incidentally, first-person monologue sermons get old quickly unless the preacher is particularly good at them and uses them infrequently! No matter how dramatic such sermons are, they remain inside the speaking character's head. Although listeners may be initially drawn in, as the sermon progresses, they are likely to feel increasingly left out—especially since they cannot talk back to the character.

8. Take the listeners on a very specific route during the sermon journey, moving deliberately (though not obviously) from one stage to the next. Every seeming aside or detour should be essential to how the sermon develops and deploys. Observations with a tenuous or a tangential connection should be cut.

9. Honor the intelligence of your listeners by shaping a space for them to draw obvious conclusions and to make their own inferences. If the preacher announces everything for the listener, the sermon becomes a monologue rather than a sacred conversation in community. Remember that the task of a sermon is to shape space rather than fill space.

10. Avoid extended quotations of all kinds, including Scripture passages, poems, and hymns. When you present a quotation, listeners overhear but do not participate. The longer a quotation goes (regardless of type or source), the less attentive listeners become. A quick paraphrase, or a crisp line selected from a quotation, will do.

11. Differentiate between the process by which you came to insight and the process by which listeners may best be able to arrive at a similar insight. Listeners need to be taken on a journey, but not necessarily (or even probably) the same one that the preacher experienced. The path you took may have included complex (even convoluted!) experiences and associations that others may not share. If you find yourself having to fill in a great deal of background material to make a point, you need to ask yourself whether there might be a more accessible route that leads to the same place.

12. Distinguish between the initial, tentative trajectory and the final, *telos* track. As you begin writing or plotting a sermon, you will be working with a tentative trajectory (a felt sense of where you are going). It is quite possible that as you get into the flow of shaping the sermon, it may develop a direction of its own. As you do final drafts, pay close attention to how the sermon has shifted from its initially projected pathway. You will probably need to trim some things and add other things as you refine the tentative trajectory into the telos track, that is, the finally formed sequence of plotted scenes and moves that make up the sermon.

13. Attend to the critical importance of introductions and conclusions. Immediately engage listeners' attention, and set it moving in a particular direction. Though the introduction need not be dramatic and should not be manipulative, it should draw listeners into an unfolding adventure rather than settling them into a passive posture. It is perfectly appropriate to change the direction of the sermon flow, but a specific focus and momentum must be established before you turn the corner. You cannot simply meander into where you are going without risking the possibility that listeners will check out and not return (or wander in and out of the sermon without really following it).

Irrelevant humor, remarks about weather, polite pleasantries, and general explanations concerning what the sermon is about are therefore seriously counterproductive. Preachers have, even with resistant listeners, a window of accessibility that lasts somewhere between thirty seconds and one minute. (Even for sympathetic listeners, we seldom have more than two minutes.) Do not squander it!

A summary seldom embodies the transforming quality of energizing grace. Appeals seldom work much better. An effective conclusion both focuses and releases the grace it describes. And stops.

It is not difficult to imagine particular circumstances or considerations that would prompt us to set aside one or another of those guidelines. Broadly, as we implement the guidelines, we follow the flow of the stage 2 sermon draft, asking these questions:

- "What is the sermon trying to say and do?"
- "What is already in the sermon that somehow gets in the way of that?"
- "What else is needed to help the sermon do that?"
- "Where and how might particular listeners have difficulty, or get derailed?"

If you find yourself asking questions like the ones that follow during this fine-tuning process, they may be a warning either that there are issues and problems needing further work at stage 2, or that you are poking unproductively at this fire:

- "How can I fix this or make that better?"
- "What would make this sound good?"
- "Where might I have to justify, defend, or protect myself?"

Preparing an Oral Manuscript for Preaching

There is another dimension of sermon preparation that preachers often pay little attention to: manuscript preparation. Mentioning this does not imply that effective preaching can be done only from a prepared text. Depending on several variables—such as the personality and preparation style of the preacher, the distinguishing characteristics of the community, the nature of the occasion, the physical features of the setting, and the structural dynamics of the sermon—full notes, limited notes, or no notes at all may be more fitting.

Congregations often appreciate being addressed by preachers who are free from notes. However, some very bad sermons are preached without notes. And sermons shared word for word from written texts can be delivered with extraordinary power. I have found that alternating those delivery modes stimulates growth in my preaching life. Preaching without text helps me craft manuscripts with more open, conversational space; preaching with text helps me discipline images, ideas, and structure when I preach extemporaneously.

Regardless of method, two ideals are at stake:

- A sense of connectedness with the congregation (not the same as showing them our impressive memorization skills)
- The sound of live conversation—language shaped for the ear of the mind, rather than the eye of the mind (and read aloud in an interesting tone of voice)

How can both ideals be achieved if we are preaching from a manuscript? Here, again, I will provide a set of suggestions with explanatory rationale. The following format will help you combine the precision of a sermon text, and the immediate congregational engagement of preaching without text:

- Put no more on a single line than your eye can comfortably pick up in one glance.

- Divide long sentences only at natural grammatical break points (for example, the beginnings of clauses, phrases, appositives, or parallel constructions).
- Begin each new sentence at the left margin.
- Indent carryover lines of sentences according to an easily identifiable pattern (for example, put parallel constructions directly under each other, or put complex sentences in descending, indented stair steps).
- Single-space text in a paragraph; double-space between paragraphs.
- Begin new paragraphs at every change of direction or momentum—much more frequently than you begin new paragraphs in essays.
- If it is helpful, further mark up the manuscript to indicate word stress, tempo, transition, mood shift, or stages in plot flow.

This format offers the following immediate advantages for delivering your sermon:

- You will not have to return every few seconds to a solid, extended block of words, and search for your place (which distracts from focusing both on your content and on your congregation). You will know exactly where to look. Your eye will instantly go to the leftmost place on the page, immediately below the line of text you last read.
- If you are beginning a new sentence, the capitalized first word at the margin will signal the need for a break and for a fresh surge of energy. If you are continuing a sentence that carries over from the previous line, the indention will signal the need to connect the phrase or clause with what has gone before (and also to present it with the appropriate energy and inflection).
- Since the text is shaped and displayed according to the rhythm of its natural energy and meaning, you will be able to concentrate more naturally on appropriate variations in pacing, volume, pitch, and speed—and on breath control.
- Your diction, without being artificial, will be more confident and energized.

113

- You will be able to spend more time with the congregation, and less time in the manuscript.

The greatest advantage of this form is not as a set of cues in the moment of delivery, but rather as a force for shaping the words you will subsequently deliver. The sermon is an oral art form, not a religious essay (even an interesting and well-read one). This format is not primarily a pattern for laying out a sermon that has already been written. It is a pattern that defines the givens and the creative possibilities of your distinctive art form.

The basic principle behind this format is simple: What your eye cannot see in a single glance, the ears of your congregation will not easily comprehend or connect, either with what has preceded or with what will follow.

The truth of this maxim is cumulative; its impact is experienced more fully the longer it is observed or disregarded. If this pattern is employed, the preaching event will be experienced as an engaging conversation between preacher and listeners, rather than as a lecture from one to the other.

This form of composition will sensitize you intuitively to the rhythms and sounds of language—what words and phrases best convey, by sound and sense, the content and tone of the message. This manner of sermon construction will even suggest specific language—words with precise and accurate connotations that you might not think of if you were composing your sermon in essay mode. An example of this sermon formatting follows:

So God goes out, and kindles a fire.
Why would God go and do that?

Why take a single bush and torch it?
Set it ablaze, without burning it up?

114

What's the point?
Seems like wasted energy.
Such a small fire,
    stuck way out there
        on the far side of the wilderness.

What could God be thinking?
Why should YHWH even care?
What good does it do?

With galaxies to energize, constellations to choreograph,
    with worlds to ignite, and worlds to incinerate,
    with shooting stars to hurl around for sheer fun,
    with all the pyrotechnic possibilities at God's disposal,
        why would God light a fire in a little bush?

The answer is so simple, it almost takes your breath away:
God does not like suffering.

———>●<———

We have been rather taken up, in the last several pages, with nuts and
bolts—bits of professional advice. But beyond a single-phrase association (*refiner's fire*), is there any deeper connection with what we
have been reflecting on here and the distinctively biblical image? We
admitted at the outset of this chapter that it stretches the fire
metaphor somewhat to describe stage 3 preparation in terms of stirring, tending, and feeding a fire that has already been built up. Have
we subjected *refiner's fire* to a similar straining, as far as the biblical
reference is concerned?

"For [God] is like a refiner's fire . . . and [God] will purify the
descendants of Levi and refine them like gold and silver, until they

present offerings to the LORD in righteousness." It sounds as though the firing Malachi has in mind is not primarily a matter of fixing their techniques as the Levites set about preparing and presenting transmissions and transactions of worship, but about what God is doing with the lives of sacred ministers—transforming them so that they can make more effective offerings.

In stage 3, we are refining our expressions of kindling art with all the professional skill we can muster as sacred wordsmiths. We are listening to what our sermons are saying back to us as preachers, about what we may (and may not) say. In our listening and wordsmithing, we are receiving the distinctive gift from God that is not a preacher's inalienable right, but certainly our particular portion of God's grace. The kind of gift I'm referring to here has nothing to do with professional competence or personal holiness, and only to do with the grace that attends a particular Christian vocation.

But something else is going on, I think. In stage 3 sermon refining, I find myself being refined. I am as achievement driven as any preacher. Yet I can testify to being subjected to God's purifying fire in the very process of focusing my attention on perfecting a sermon as fully as I can. It is not a mechanical procedure—changing a specific word does not necessarily help purify a particular place in my life (although there is often a connection between getting clear on what I need to say, and becoming clearer on whom God is calling me to become). More often, it has to do with feeling that as I listen for ways to articulate the piercing, sweet sound of amazing grace, I am remade. Listening as a kindling artist for God's word through me, I hear God's word to me.

7

Coming to Cast Fire, Versus Calling Down Fire

When the days drew near for him to be taken up, he set his face to go to Jerusalem. And he sent messengers ahead of him. On their way they entered a village of the Samaritans to make ready for him; but they did not receive him, because his face was set toward Jerusalem. When his disciples James and John saw it, they said, "Lord, do you want us to command fire to come down from heaven and consume them?" But he turned and rebuked them. (Luke 9:51–55)

"I came to bring fire to the earth, and how I wish it were already kindled!" (Luke 12:49)

In a sobering synchronicity, I began drafting this chapter on the first day of my country's first recent preemptive war. Invoking the blessing of God in a cosmic moral contest against a nation he branded as evil, our president, George W. Bush, committed the might of the U.S. military in a crusade to depose Iraq's leadership, find and destroy its weapons of mass destruction, and liberate its people. Missile explosions, massive fireballs, and burning buildings illuminated the landscape of Baghdad. The ultimate costs of the forces unleashed by the U.S. fighters remain incalculable. The United States embarked on a course of action that can be described at many levels as playing with fire. An escalating exchange of incendiary rhetoric over months and years had led inexorably to the release of incendiary weapons wreaking massive destruction. (The distinction between the United States' weapons of massive destruction and Iraq's weapons of mass destruction was probably lost on those hit by the fires.)

James, that old curmudgeon Epistle writer (who, "being dead, yet speaketh"), says, "How great a forest is set ablaze by a small fire! And the tongue is a fire" (James 3:5b-6a, NRSV). In the months following the tragic ignitings of the World Trade Center towers, the Pentagon, and a field in Pennsylvania, the president frequently turned to what is sometimes termed "preacher language." He issued moral condemnations, exhorted his compatriots to courageous resolve, and signed off major addresses enjoining God to "continue to bless America." He confidently invoked the justice of God as a justification for his determination of national policy, in which war became an offensive strategic policy instead of a final defensive expedient. Along the road to war, the president demonstrated unswerving resolve and sincere conviction. So did James and John, "the Sons of Thunder," whom Jesus had summoned into disciple service.

The scene Luke sets is charged with political tension. Jesus is passing through Samaria, headed for Jerusalem ("his face," Luke says, is "set" in that direction). A Samaritan village is asked for hospitality—and refuses to give it. James and John are outraged. Remembering their history (somewhat selectively), they invoke the example of their ancestor Elijah: "Lord, do you want us to call down fire from heaven and consume them?" (forgetting, apparently, the unintended chain of events that employing a scorched-altar policy set in motion for Elijah). The response Jesus makes to their indignant request is swift and clear: "He turned and rebuked them." There is a sermon in there for those who seek to call down fire. As intimated earlier, to depict the vocation of preaching as playing with fire is to employ ambivalent metaphors.

When I was a child, an itinerant evangelist came to our small Kentucky town for a week of revival services. Jokes are often cracked about hellfire-and-damnation preachers; this was no joke. The preacher warmed to his task with vigor. In graphic detail, he com-

118

pared the fate of unsaved sinners to that of the victims of a recent hotel fire. His audience listened with rapt attention. His preaching got results. In response to an altar call, people streamed down the aisles. My father, the local pastor, baptized almost two hundred souls on the following two Sunday nights—an athletic feat of no small significance, since he was a Baptist who practiced full immersion. You might think that the ranks of the church were thereby swelled with scores of new converts; but once having been baptized, none of those folks ever came to church again—in spite of earnest entreaties in pastoral follow-up calls.

People are often burned by preaching in ways less blatant but no less painful. Under the rubric of preaching judgment, preachers of differing persuasions issue all manner of edicts and threats, taking on the difficult but necessary duty of afflicting the comfortable, and justifying their approach as telling it like it is—expressing tough love. The life-transforming potential that comes through speaking hard truth is lost under the threatening gestures of preachers who all the while protest that they'd rather not have to say these hard things, or that the messages also apply to them.

Sometimes preachers are not directly responsible for the incendiary effects of their language. Words they labor to say clearly and kindly occasionally explode in people whose difficult life circumstances (unknown to the preachers) create conditions where a spark, intended as insight, produces conflagration. (At times that happens because of residual wounds from abusive sermons heard years before.)

In light of the devastation touched off by the fiery language of politicians and preachers, there might well be a word to the author of a book with the title *Playing with Fire*: Preaching as playing with fire? You don't want to go there. The problem is—Jesus does. Or so it seems.

Not three chapters later in Luke's Gospel, after having expressly forbidden James and John to call down fire, Jesus says, "I came to cast fire upon the earth, and how I wish it were already kindled!"

119

Having just squelched the pyromania-prone tendencies of his Sons of Thunder associates, Jesus now appears eager to do precisely what he has told them not to do! What is the difference between coming to cast fire and calling it down?

One thing can be said with certainty: preaching as play, as we have been describing it, is not, by implication, making nice. Bestowing bland platitudes or blessing all that moves befits a preacher no better than hurling thunderbolt invectives. There has never been a preaching ministry exempt from the necessity of telling hard and timely truths. When? How? What may seem called for is a list of hard-truth occasions: "In these situations you mustn't preach difficult truths; in those you may; in these you must!" But relying on such a list would be both impossible and too easy. Such a list could never cover all cases. If it did, it might imply that, in "must" cases, preachers could simply say what they believe and walk away, letting the chips fall, shaking the dust from their feet. They can't.

"Shall we call down fire and consume them?" ask James and John. "I have come to cast fire on the earth," says Jesus. The two situations Luke so closely juxtaposes are not as similar as they seem. James and John are bent on incinerating the axis of evil du jour (as they see it): "They are obstructing Our Holy Purpose! They need to be taken out, so that we can get on with our mission!" Jesus says no. (Just before this event, he also rebuked John, who wanted to silence an exorcist "because he does not follow us." Undercutting invidious "us-them" distinctions, Jesus simply says, "Whoever is not against you is for you.")

The fire Jesus brings to the earth, on the other hand, does not burn anyone, though it does have serious implications for him: "I have a baptism to be baptized with, and how constrained I am until it is accomplished." The context of Jesus's proclamation involves the fire of passionate self-sacrificing commitment, of centering insight, a fire that burns away imperfections that inhibit the in-breaking power of the Commonwealth of God. There is a world of difference between an incinerating fire—one that wounds, reduces to ashes—and a cauterizing, purifying fire. The difference is not in where the fire is lit, but in why it is brought down and how it burns. Perhaps preachers, especially in the presence of so many mis-ignited, incinerating fires, need continually to fight fire with fire. But if we do, it is incumbent on us to build our fires without getting caught up in what we seek to check. (Feeling passionate about what we preach is not a reliable indicator that the fires we build are cleansing fires, that what we intend for healing does not function as holocaust.)

How can proper intentionality be manifested in method and carried out in practice? First let us appropriate a vision of what it means to preach God's judgment, and then let us set forth strategies to inform sermon preparation with that vision. Robert Capon, who writes about metaphorical theology, compares the four last things (death, judgment, hell, and heaven) to the four seasons. Two of his comparisons are obvious: death is winter; hell is summer. His third comparison is not as immediately apparent, but makes good sense upon reflection: heaven is autumn—the season of vibrant color, ingathered fruits, fulfillment. That leaves, by default, what seems an utter mismatch: judgment is spring! What connection can there be between a falling gavel, announcing a death sentence, and the rising green of returning life?

Ah! says Capon, anticipating our sense of disconnect: that simply shows how deeply we misunderstand the judgment of God! Judgment is not synonymous with condemnation, penalty, punishment—the infliction of shame or suffering. Human judgment (both condemnation of self and demonization of others) often means exactly those; God's judgment never does. The judgment of God is always discernment, and discernment is an activity of naming, differentiating what is unhealthy and healthy, what is dead (needing to be pruned) and what is alive (needing to be nourished). Spring, concludes Capon, is the seasonal celebration of discernment. After the long winter, when everything seems dead, we are able to discern what is really alive. We can discern the difference between one form of plant life and another—and honor the distinctions appropriately (Robert Farrar Capon, *The Youngest Day: Shelter Island's Seasons in the Light of Grace*, San Francisco: Harper and Row, 1983).

If "neither do I condemn you" is what Jesus said to the woman taken in adultery (after sharp interaction with her accusers that resulted in sparks of insight showering in all directions), then it is hard to imagine ourselves, as preachers, rushing in where Jesus will not tread! Yet if Jesus's words do not condemn, neither do they condone, for discerning words do neither.

If judgment is discernment, then gone is any valid satisfaction (or any justified reticence) in telling the congregation a thing or two. Gone, as well, are the comfort and guilt in simply letting sleeping dogs lie. Preachers are called, like the One they follow, to cast fire on the earth—to light up the planet, to show things for what they are—to name the world as they find it, in beauty, tragedy, sin, grace, and hope. All the energy that we marshal in giving our listeners what-for can be channeled toward looking and listening, then shaping and speaking, so that those among whom we preach will themselves be able to see and hear (and speak and shape). If there is no condemnation but rather conviction to be brought by the Spirit, our task as preachers is not to stand in for the Spirit's work, but to prepare a place for the Spirit to come. The basic play strategies described in chapters 4–6 intend precisely this; but in the particular context of preaching judgment—preaching discernment—some more specific strategies can be suggested:

Make generous use of descriptive language, minimal use of prescriptive language. When evaluative language is employed (particularly language loaded with negative assessment), listeners are seldom given space to arrive for themselves at the assessment the preacher is advancing. In public worship, where convention dictates that talking back is socially inappropriate, even listeners otherwise open to a preacher's assessments may feel trapped, muzzled, given no say.

If the issue under consideration is complex, controversial, or resistant to quick resolution, listeners may feel that their preacher is taking inappropriate advantage of a privileged speaking space—is even guilty of an abuse of power. If listeners feel that their behaviors or motives are under attack, or that their preacher is pushing as a Gospel imperative the opposite side of an issue on which they have considered convictions, they will dig in deeper where they already are. It is not clear that such reactions give preachers license to "shake the dust off their feet."

This suggestion is a straightforward translation of the vision we have just outlined (with help from Capon). The language of description is the language of discerning judgment; the language of prescription is the language of condemning judgment—explicit or implied. It is only a short step from the moral finger-pointing language of "we must," "we ought," "we should" to the conclusion, "God will condemn if you don't clean up." It is hard for listeners to distance their experience of such encounters from unpleasant encounters with parents, teachers, bosses, and police officers, regardless of whether those confrontations were justified.

Instructive, is it not, how the prophet Nathan confronts David with God's judgment over his adultery with Bathsheba and subsequent murder of her loyal soldier-husband? Every word Nathan uses, as he tells David the story of a rich man's stealing of a poor family's lamb, is indicative, rather than imperative. Nathan simply names what is—describing the unfolding dynamics of the situation in vivid word pictures. There is no invective, only announcement, giving David space to make his own judgment about the covenant with death that his actions have cut (2 Sam 11–12:15).

A close reading of Israel's prophets (Isaiah, Jeremiah, Ezekiel, Hosea, and Amos, among others) shows (perhaps surprisingly) that, while they speak in no uncertain terms, they employ language more to name than to blame. The same is true, of course, of the teaching of Jesus, not only in the parables but also in the discourses. Even when Jesus plunges into full-scale controversy, the preponderance of language is telling it like it is rather than telling folks to go to hell (even in the classic sheep-and-goats parable of Matthew, chapter 25). When he pronounces, "Woe to you, scribes and Pharisees—hypocrites!" his words have the character of a desperate last-minute warning—and they are spoken more in sorrow than in anger (note how he weeps like a child when his attempts fall on deaf ears).

If those senior preaching colleagues found in the Scriptures can do that, so can we; we can at least train our language in their direction. It is instructive to review the texts of hellfire-and-damnation sermons. The vivid invectives they contain tend to be little more than brandished moral abstractions. Conspicuously absent from such sermons is any attempt to present the complexities and dynamics of sin, grace, urgency, and possibility in descriptive terms. Preachers who hurl incendiary moral missiles thereby indicate that they have not done their homework.

The concern raised here is not restricted to preachers of any particular theological stripe. Urbane liberal preachers can be just as infected as fundamentalist preachers. Often, listeners withdraw self-protectively from clearly recognizable missile strikes. Those listening to more sophisticated forms of condemnation may not know what hit them until after the preaching event—and even then may not be fully conscious of what has happened.

Hard words may need to be said. Delicate laser surgery may need to be performed for the spiritual health of a community. However, that kind of careful judgment does not look much like what I saw over Baghdad on television. The two forms of judgment have little in common. Discerning description achieves, through the agency of God's Spirit and the freedom of listener response, what condemning prescription (in its sincere form) actually intends. Prescriptive judgment seldom achieves what it sets out to do—especially over the long term.

This has nothing to do with being soft on sin, or refusing to undertake difficult, even unpopular responsibility. It does have to do with the kind of saying exactly what we see that is at the heart of truly prophetic speaking. Fred Craddock's oft-invoked adage fits well here: "The important thing in preaching is not to get something said, but to get something heard." The former is radically vulnerable to becoming a rationalized venting of frustration. The latter comes as an insight that the listener hears inside and scarcely recognizes as coming from the preacher at all. Robin Meyers reminds us succinctly: No one ever convinces anyone else of anything. All communicators can do is to provide listeners with the resources by which those listeners may be able to convince themselves (see Robin R. Meyers, *With Ears to Hear: Preaching as Self-Persuasion*, Cleveland: Pilgrim Press, 1993).

Make generous use of evocative language, minimal use of exhorting language. I have a colleague who tells her preaching students she does not want to hear salad sermons—sermons filled with, "Let us do this; let us do that!" A frequent variant on this preacher-as-cheerleader speech pattern is, "We are called to . . . " As a way of seeming not to be bossy or presumptuous, preachers sometimes preface what they want their congregations to feel, think, or do by saying, "I don't know about you, but I . . . " All these phrases are words of exhortation—intended not so much to issue moral pronouncements as to encourage moral action. Clearly, preaching intends not only to hold up a mirror for self-discernment, but also to raise talismans and lead spirited charges. The Gospel, well preached and heard, does not leave us or let us stay where we are.

There is, however, a distinction to be made (hard to define, but not difficult to recognize) between speech that drives people forward and speech that calls people forth—naming and releasing an empowering sense of vision and action. Describing an emerging direc-

125

tion—naming it a sin process already, born of scarcely recognized Spirit-infused resources—that will get a community much further down the road than rehearsing what they must do next.

Demonstrate compassionate understanding for the position of the other. Whether the hard word we feel we must say is directed toward a social-political orientation (say, the interwoven idolatries of the military state and the consumer self), or toward an internal disposition of human character (for example, a self-destructive refusal to forgive), it is important not to demonize those (including ourselves) who may well be enslaved by forces beyond human control.

There are two good reasons for dealing, however decisively, nevertheless gently with all who have gone astray. The first: As the Epistle writer sagely observes, "We wrestle not against flesh and blood, but against principalities and powers" (Eph 6:12). The first strategic tack employed by those insidious forces is to vent our fear and frustration against their power by targeting particular individuals and groups for denunciation, and projecting our own demons on others (or even vilifying ourselves). To be sucked into that demonic deception is to participate unwittingly in their destructive work. To call down fire on the other rather than coming to cast fire on the earth.

The second: Real though it is, evil is good gone sour, a cleverly contrived counterfeit of what is, at root, God's good gift. Addictions would not be so attractive were not the inherent creaturely dynamics of hunger and satisfaction an integral part of a created order that God called into being and pronounced very good. "War is healthy and fun!" an acquaintance of mine was told recently by a soldier spoiling for fight in Iraq. While that sentiment all but takes my breath away, it is critical for me to remember that the values of courage, struggle, and achievement in the face of grave danger are, in fact, important ways in which humans bear witness to God's implanted image.

For both of those reasons, dealing with evil needs to begin not just with the blanket abstract assertion that no one is exempt from

126

temptation, but also with a careful, appreciative analysis of that which is healthy in what has become infected. Gracefully empowering speech begins not in self-righteous excoriation, but in compassionate celebration. Why does what is so ultimately destructive seem so attractive? That needs to be our place of departure. Why do those who behave as they do find it so right? What is genuinely plausible (and thus so deceiving) in what they—we—intend?

Avoid summarily depicting alternative stances of thought and action in emotionally charged categories of either/or, and good/evil. It must have felt energizing for Elijah, and for James and John, to urge what they may have regarded as a reiteration of Moses's classic drawing-a-line-in-the-sand speech: "Behold, I have set before you life and death, blessing and cursing, therefore choose life." It feels similar, I suspect, when circumstances combine to stir up fire-and-brimstone dispositions in us. Herein, however, lies exhibit A of the counterfeit danger just alluded to. We are charged, as preachers, with the task of critical discernment: naming wheat and tares for what they are, sorting out good fish from bad fish, differentiating fine pearls from fake ones, wise ways of waiting for a long-delayed bridegroom from foolish ones. In our own ways of encountering those who are marginalized, we need to note our tendencies toward sheeplike and goatlike behaviors. Yet . . . it is precisely because such distinctions are so difficult to make that preacher-mentor Matthew depicts them so graphically.

I'll never forget a preaching conference for seminarians I helped to conduct some years ago. The students held a wide spectrum of theological opinions, but they were engaging one another with attention and respect. The community of preachers was forming effectively. A guest speaker began her presentation. She happened to be an incendiary liberal. A striking figure—wheelchair bound—she was an effective street warrior for social justice, taking courageous positions of advocacy with articulate passion. In her presentation to us on that particular day, however, she lobbed firebombs, one after another, against conservative theological positions, some of which were thoughtfully and conscientiously held by a number of participants. To gracious, respectful questions from those individuals, she responded with repeated ad hominem attacks.

The collegial atmosphere became suddenly guarded. Later that evening, defending the speaker (whom he had invited), a prominent bishop told those in the conservative seminaries (explicitly named) that they were going to have to get with the program, or find themselves left out of the church. I suspect you can imagine the impact of his words. We who were responsible for conducting the conference watched helplessly as our careful planning for communal work went down in flames.

As divine providence would have it, our speaker on the following morning was Walter Brueggemann, who arrived knowing nothing of the conference dynamics. In he strode—shining bald head, deep raspy voice, burning coal eyes. In ten minutes, he deftly described the failure of both liberal and conservative theologians to take deeply to heart the witness of the Hebrew Scriptures to a liberating God. He proceeded to outline strategies that all of us could employ to prepare a way for God's in-breaking Righteous Realm. The impact was as dramatically positive as the one from previous day had been negative.

In issues where there is sincere disagreement, seek points of reference manifesting common commitment. This is exactly what Brueggemann did for our conference. It is also what my own rector did in the sermon she offered on the Sunday after the drafting of this chapter began—the Sunday after the beginning of the U.S. war in Iraq. Her sermon began with a question: "Since war has begun, what will we do now?" She acknowledged that people had prayed, written, spoken, and demonstrated both in opposition to and in support of the war. Yet all of that is now, she said, like watercolor paints on a canvas—unalterable, once applied. The question, then, is, "What will we make of this canvas now?" Working from the texts of the Scriptures appointed for the day (the Ten Commandments, Paul's "wretched man that I am" in Romans 7:24, and Jesus's cleansing of the Temple in John 2:13ff.), she spoke candidly of the inherently contentious character of the human condition—and of the subversive peace strategies we could undertake, beginning with the relationship that the parish had recently initiated with our neighbors in a nearby Islamic weekend school.

Rather than telling listeners what to think or do, seek words, images, and courses of action that help listeners articulate what they deeply long to affirm. Rather than speaking at or talking to congregations, preachers need to consciously make verbal offerings to God, ones that speak for and with the congregation, giving them voices they can recognize as their own (though they might not have thought of putting things those ways). This involves more than simply shifting from the pronoun *you* to the pronoun *I*. It requires long-term listening, drawing on what has been heard and shared over the entire length of a pastoral relationship. Trying, on the spur of the moment, to adopt such a stance is akin to trying to be a best friend to those we don't know well when their lives have been struck by tragedy.

Imagine yourself as someone being addressed by your sermon. Jesus's two-sided summary of the Law is as much a matter of homiletical-spiritual methodology for preachers as it is a precept for them to put forward. Indeed, the Law of Love is probably more effectively conveyed by the manner in which we embody the principle in our preaching than by the words we employ when we talk about it.

Cast language to convey a sense of conversation, not pronouncement. An image that interplays for me with that of the fire and smoke over Baghdad is of the formal press conference conducted by President Bush not many days before the threat became reality. Reporters framed thoughtful questions. The atmosphere was respectful. However, almost every question was dodged, or addressed only obliquely. The president stayed on message, making pronouncements concerning long-formulated administration positions. Issues raised by reporters were never specifically met. The evening was a monologue, punctuated by an occasional opening for the sound of another voice, which served only as a prompt for whatever the speaker wished to say. Whatever the occasion was, it was not a conference.

When hard words need to be said, the preacher cannot stand six feet above contradiction. It is not necessary—indeed it is counterproductive—to turn any sermon, especially a difficult one, into a town meeting. What does have to take place, however, is a deliberate attempt to shape the sermon as a serious conversation space.

Write your way into warm detachment. This suggestion came from a woman participating in a conference for preachers in the Church of England as we strategized about effective ways of kindling the fire of discernment. Though I know how many drafts a sermon may take, and have journalized through difficult issues, I had never put the two experiences together. All we observed in the last chapter on stage 3 preparation becomes especially important when we are dealing with conflictive and complex issues. The difference in how I sound from the pulpit may well be made by my willingness to feel my way, through pencil and paper, or computer and screen, from passions so close to me that I cannot effectively express them, to passions I can more healthily enkindle, striking a spark on waiting tinder rather than blasting away with a blowtorch.

Part of my intensity may have to do not so much with my clarity and righteousness of vision, as with the intense anxiety that often precedes arriving at a centered expression of articulate vision. What a tragedy if, under the self-deceived guise of prophetic passion, I actually dispensed upon a captive audience my own spiritual and artistic frustration!

Engage the texts of the Scriptures as sources of deep theological resonance with conditions listeners are facing, rather

than as proof texts for particular stances. The suggestions for stage 1 preparation that were offered in chapter 4 become particularly important for sermons that need to set forth a difficult discerning word. There is a strong tendency either to select a Scripture passage or to seek in the Scriptures for an answer we think our listeners need to hear (even though, as in the press conference, it may be an answer to questions nobody is asking!). But, as we have said, the Word of the God, as found in the Scriptures, is seldom, if ever, "Now hear this!" What is actually going on in the texts we are engaging? The situation there will not be just like that which we are facing. But there may be surprising points of contact that can shift the point of reference for discerning where God's fire may alight to cleanse and heal our situation.

Envision the difference between words that burn people at the stake, and words that create an altar space for the descent of holy, cleansing fire. That, obviously, is not a simple method for extinguishing bad-fire phrases and striking up good-fire alternatives in sermon manuscripts. The difference between a fire that comes down and consumes and a fire cast upon the earth to cleanse is determined by context, not driven by rule. Yet imaginal orientation has more practical import in sermon shaping than we might think. Simply (as a last check) looking over one's hard-word-of-discernment sermon and asking, "Of those two alternatives, which does my sermon sound, look, and feel more like?" will have value as a spiritual exercise, and may make a difference.

I was not able to spend much time in front of the television during the bombing of Baghdad. Yet, during the few moments I did face the devastating spectacle, I observed in myself a certain fascination. What to make of that? At one level, I suspect, it was a manifestation of the rubberneck phenomenon. Regardless of how grisly an event, there is a spontaneous desire to see it firsthand rather than settle for a secondhand report. Television does provide a detached, seemingly safe place from which to stay in touch with what is going on. (And thus it dulls our discrimination even as it stimulates our senses.)

But I believe there was another reason for my fascination. I realized that what I saw had a certain beauty—not entirely unlike the awesome effect of a spectacular Fourth of July fireworks display. As I thought of that, I also realized that behind the horrific scenes, countless acts of courage, skill, compassion, and sacrifice were being undertaken by participants on both sides of the tragedy. The cooperative human creativity involved in effecting weapons of massive destruction is awesome as well as awful. The war in Baghdad was playing with fire in the worst senses of the phrase *playing with fire*, and in many of its best senses also. War does bring out the best as well as the worst in people. And that reminds me afresh that such destructive forces are prime examples of evil as a counterfeit—good gone sour. The light of the original Eden and the light of the new Jerusalem stand in discerning judgment over the lurid firelight we hurl at each other. The energies making for healthy play—freedom, community, adventure, and creativity—are essential for the very forces that parody and undermine the healthy play of God's creation. To that horror, no preacher can be passive. Having chosen to accept our calling, on occasion, with carefully crafted strategy, we fight fire with fire. The danger is that we can be seduced into playing with fire in ways like those now suffered by the world, rather than in ways that God intends.

8

Alighting on Each of Them

When the day of Pentecost had come, they were all together in one place. And suddenly from heaven there came a sound like the rush of a violent wind, and it filled the entire house where they were sitting. Divided tongues, as of fire, appeared among them, and a tongue rested on each of them. And all of them were filled with the Holy Spirit and began to speak in other languages, as the Spirit gave them ability. (Acts of the Apostles 2:1–4)

As a language student in high school, I was less than stellar; French and Latin did not come easily. When Luke's account of the day of Pentecost was read aloud in church, I listened with envy-laced incredulity. How lucky could a language student get! Peter, Andrew, James, and John didn't have to plod through the grammar and vocabulary of Parthian, Median, Elamite, or Mesopotamian. Painless language learning—a miracle too good to be true! As an amateur theologian in midlife, I have a different take on that biblical text. Something miraculous did occur, I am convinced; but now I see the mystery of Pentecost as less magical and more momentous.

The feast of Pentecost was an annual event in Jerusalem. Every year, "devout Jews from every nation under heaven" (Acts 2:5) gathered to celebrate the giving of the Law, held by tradition to have taken place seven weeks after Passover. What glorious chaos the mingling of voices must have made! Almost like Babel, and yet its an-

133

tithesis: the one true God worshiped by a mighty multiethnic chorus—meaning dancing through an orchestra of different language
forms. How much would the disciples know of Parthian, Median,
Elamite, and Mesopotamian? "Nothing," I suspect they would say.

But you can't rub shoulders with folks for years without some of
their words and ways rubbing off on you. The sound of conversation
in other tongues was background noise at best. But what goes on at
the periphery of consciousness is present, nonetheless. Remember
those chariots of fire around Elisha that his servant couldn't see until
his eyes were opened?

My imagination now fills in the spaces of Luke's narrative in a
different way than once it did. There are disciples, gathered in prayer,
waiting for a promised something, they know not what. Spiritual energy explodes on them. It has been gathering force since the Resurrection. Today it comes to critical mass. Tongues of fire—that's as
close a description as Luke can find: "Divided tongues, as of fire, appeared among them, and a tongue rested on each of them." What do
any of these disciples have by way of language skills? Probably no
more than the equivalent of five loaves and two fishes. But that is all
the Spirit needs. Somehow what has enlightened the disciples to
God's freedom, community, adventure, and creativity simply has to
find its way into explicit focus through all these different languages.
Leaping across linguistic barriers, tongues of fire begin to spread.

How, exactly? In my imagination's ear, I hear Peter (taking
charge, as usual): "Andrew, go to the Parthians! Thomas, take the
Medes! James and John, you Thunder Boys know a bit of Elamite; go
mix with them! Bartholomew, Nathaniel, Matthew, find some
dwellers of Mesopotamia and start a conversation as best you can!"
Their command of vocabulary and grammar is very limited. Their
speech is broken at best. What they have to share is utterly beyond
their ability. But, truth be told, what they have to share can't be articulated in their own native tongue either. So what do they have to

lose, when everyone has so much to gain? Off they go. Out tumble Spirit-fired phrases—points of contact with another culture that aim beyond themselves to the one God who is in and above them all. Sentences are garbled. Syntax is such as to make rhetoricians wince. The hermeneutical skills of these disciple-interpreters leave much to be desired. But the Spirit isn't proud; the Spirit just works with what the Spirit is given (the Spirit always does). Great gaps of meaning open up as the poor preachers scramble to communicate. The disciples don't know the words for most of what they want to share. The words they do have often miscast the creative, communal, adventuring, liberating Love they are trying to convey. Just listen! Sheer cacophony! Nothing coherent can come from this, let alone anything fruitful!

But, listen again. Do you hear what I hear? Those to whom the disciples are preaching are not simply standing around listening passively! They are asking questions, suggesting alternative phrases for what they don't get or can't quite follow ("Is this what you are trying to say?"). They are recasting matters in ways that make sense to them. They are checking out their hearings. They are challenging the amazing claims they are hearing. From those who are preaching to them, the listeners are drawing out expressions and insights that those preachers didn't know they knew. All are encountering one another (and their common God) in the dynamic matrix of surging, pulsing Spirit-ed conversation. Do you see what I see? Everyone is playing with fire—sparks are flying in all directions. This is what the playing-with fire is supposed to be like—the antidote to the incinerating fire that some disciples so recently sought to call down.

This fire is not the property of the designated fire bringers! Eldad and Medad have, at last, found a voice in the Parthians and the Medes. "Would that all God's people were prophets!" Moses told an anxious Joshua once upon a time, as flames were fostered by uncertified fire tenders (Num 11:29). When Moses said it, it seemed no more than wishful thinking. (After bursting out in prophecy once, you re-

135

member, Eldad and Medad "did so no more.") Moses's fond ideal has finally become reality in a way that the original observer of the burning bush could never have imagined.

It takes a congregation to make a sermon—a congregation speaking back to its preacher. Saying "Amen!" perhaps, but sometimes saying, "Step on up!" or, "Help that messenger, God!" And then proceeding, by the Spirit, to active participation in the Spirit's answer to their petition. You have found this true, have you not, in your own preaching? Someone comes up after the sermon (which left much to be desired) and thanks you with tears for saying exactly what she or he needed to hear (and you know you said no such thing.) Or a handshaker at the door, in a pithy phrase, picks up where your sermon left off, and finishes it in a way you profoundly wish you had! That's the speaking back—every bit as much Spirit inspired as the words that went forth from you as designated preacher of the day.

Well, that's the kind of thing I envision going on in the silent, open spaces Luke leaves, or perhaps puts, in his Pentecost story. With respect to their subsequent testimony, Luke is explicit about those whose attentions were captured by Pentecost preaching: "[I]n our own languages, we hear them speaking about God's deeds of power!" (Acts 2:11), Luke has the citizens of Pontus, Phrygia, and Pamphylia say. But concerning how the message was transmitted, Luke is less precise: "All of them were filled with the Holy Spirit and they began to speak in other languages, as the Spirit gave them ability." (Not unlike what we see in each Gospel account, when a limited supply of bread that is blessed, broken, and shared by Jesus becomes more than enough for all.)

This is not, please note, a demythologized reading of the Scripture text ("We all know there has to be a perfectly natural explanation—it probably happened like this . . . "). I am convinced that what happened at Pentecost could have come about by no means other than the direct infusing of Spirit fire. (Just as I am convinced that no amount of exegesis, hermeneutics, and playful sermon plotting will, on its own, make an effective sermon.) But I am suggesting that the Spirit's work at Pentecost did not consist in the presentation of solo performers to an assembly of passive auditors. Pentecost is the outpouring of the Spirit on, and the convening by the Spirit of, what we have come to call the church—the community of Spirit-ed conversation, a powerful, generative expression of God's sacred play.

But the text doesn't say that. My interpretation is a worthwhile dream in an eschatological vision of preaching, perhaps; but is it Luke's? Good question; but let's leave it for the moment (with a promise to take it up again). For now, let's ask what the people of God might look like if they lived into Moses's vision: "Would that all God's people were prophets and preachers!" And how, in view of what we have said about the kindling art of preaching, we might be able to move toward that ideal. How can everyone within the community of faith (and some who don't even thus identify themselves) help preaching happen? Whether our primary place is the pulpit or the pew, all of us are engaged in preaching. How can we, regardless of role, effectively listen to, reflect on, and talk about the sermons we hear? That question has everything to do with what it means to be people of the Word. It is, however, easier asked than answered; for if we encourage such speaking back, we will quickly discover that preaching discussion can easily become captive to speech patterns that characterize other discussion groups in which we have probably engaged. Let me name, by way of image, the marks of some such groups:

- *Fan clubs*. Where star performers are indiscriminately applauded
- *TV talk shows*. Where strong convictions are tossed out (or shot from the hip)
- *Political focus / market research groups*. Where ideas are tested for popularity

137

- *Therapy/support groups*. Where members offer one another affirmation
- *Speech contests / jury deliberations*. Where ratings are given, verdicts are rendered
- *Advisory committees*. Where job performances are reviewed and critiqued

It can be difficult to keep from adopting the patterns of those groups. Their characteristic behaviors are modeled for us constantly. We do not easily shed experiences we have had in such groups when we convene to talk about preaching. The patterns are ready to hand, ingrained. If we fall into them, however, our conversations will produce predictable, unfruitful responses, such as these:

- *"You're so GOOD!"* If we function as a fan club (And yet, of course, it is not the purpose of a sermon simply to call forth delight in a preacher's skill, or to evoke praise for a job well done.)
- *"Well, my opinion is . . . !"* If we operate in TV talk show mode (Though it may be hoped that preaching will generate responses, even conflicting ones, the point of preaching is not primarily to stir things up.)
- *"This will sell; but that won't fly!"* If we behave as though we were a political focus group or a market research group (Imagine how much of the proclamation found in the Scriptures would have made it into the canon if it had been selected by public opinion!)
- *"Thanks so much for sharing; we affirm you in your journey!"* If our reflections take the shape of a therapy or support group (Preaching is personal, but it's not about the preacher.)
- *"You win!"/"You lose!"* If our observations are framed as decisions of a judge or jury (Although snap judgments are common in public discourse, something other than a thumbs-up or a thumbs-down is required in response to what is offered in a sermon.)
- *"We'll fix it for you!"* If our group perceives itself as an advisory

committee (Suggestions for improvement will be welcome in due course, but to issue summary performance assessments is to misperceive our role as conversation participants.)

When we convene as a group of sermon listeners, we do not gather just to be nice to the preacher, to exchange pious sentiments, to sniff out tendencies toward heresy, to administer criticism for the preacher's own good. When we gather for preaching discernment, our primary identity is that of a community of covenant listeners in Spirit-ed conversation. That identity grounds and connects us whether we are preacher, respondent, or group facilitator. More is required than operation according to principles of healthy group dynamics. We gather as expectant listeners for the Word of God—as that comes through the words we share with each other. We ground our exchanges in the pattern of divine revelation and human response that animates the whole of the Judeo-Christian tradition. We come together in reverent celebration around God's Holy Fire.

Preaching is not a solo performance by the one in the pulpit or a spectator sport for those in the pew. In an Episcopal understanding of the Eucharist, the celebrant convenes the community, and leads it in the Great Thanksgiving, but does not make the sacrament happen. Christ is deemed sacramentally present to a community in bread and wine only if the Eucharistic prayer is offered by at least two or three gathered together in his name. In like manner, a sermon is not simply a speech composed and delivered by a single preacher. A sermon is a preaching event unfolding in the spaces and interactions between preachers and listeners. A conversation is always going on when preaching occurs—even though congregational responses may not be audible (consisting, perhaps, in no more than thoughts such as, "This is boring; I am out of here!"). What role can the congregation play? A three-stage one:

1. Conversational listening with the preacher before the event
2. Active, informed listening during the event
3. Discerning, mutual listening with the preacher after the event

Congregations are expected to listen to the preacher during sermon delivery, but are seldom invited to listen with the preacher beforehand or afterward. Perhaps it is no wonder that injunctions to listen are sometimes less than effective! Congregational participation is likely to be more effective during the sermon if it is enlisted and engaged throughout the entire preaching process. Full congregations can seldom gather before and after the Sunday sermon, but representatives can—in accordance with principles like the ones that follow.

1. Conversational Listening with the Preacher Before the Event

A community sermon preparation is not a theological free-for-all. Just passing the microphone around does not guarantee a sermon conversation; it may shut such conversation down. Those who gather to help a preacher by listening to an upcoming sermon need a nurturing space to express what they deeply hear. The sharing of contrasting, even conflicting perspectives is essential to vital sermon speech. But when we gather to discern the Word of God, something is going on other than personal affirmation, conflict management, or dealing with the wounds of inner children. Nor is *sermon preparation community* merely pious nomenclature for a gathering of guinea pigs (though it may provide insights for a preacher on how best to proceed). What might a Spirit-ed conversation pattern look like in the community preparation of a sermon?

1. Careful, prayerful, repeated readings of the assigned Scripture lessons by all participants before the group is convened
2. A period of silent centering and focusing prayer after the group have gathered and greeted one another

140

3. An oral, meditative reading of the text, followed by silence and then another reading
4. A succinct naming of images, issues, actions, tensions, and questions present in, or directly connected with, the Scripture text, that have caught the various attentions of gathered participants
   - These sharings should be focused in single sentences, and recorded visibly.
   - No participant should offer more than one observation at a time.
   - This naming should be conducted without discussion, except insofar as an observation by one participant triggers an observation by another.
   - The preacher may facilitate and record, but should not actively participate.
5. An additional oral, meditative reading of the text
6. A naming—as in step 4—of concerns in these areas:
   - The congregation
   - The community
   - National and international affairs
7. A brief presentation by the preacher (perhaps with a succinct handout) of historical, theological, and literary dimensions of the text relevant to deep, contextual listening (as distinct from an initial, spontaneous hearing)
8. The following question, posed for interactive discussion: "What do we need to hear through a sermon in light of our listening to the Scriptures, to the stories of our own lives, and to the circumstances that we face as a community?" (The preacher may now take a more active role, but primarily as one who evokes an interchange of ideas, images, feelings, and experiences—contributing to, but not controlling, the discussion.)
9. An integrating summary of the sense of the meeting, or of the distinctive issue currents that have surfaced in the conversation
10. A brainstorming session in which images, insights, and obser-

vations of potential sermon relevance are offered. (This discussion is not an attempt to arrive at consensus, or to fix the preacher's sermon problem. Rather, it is a sharing of resources to seed the preacher's vision. If a communal sense of specific sermon strategies or shapes emerges from this discussion, that is fine, but it is not the intent of the session—the intent is to open things up for the preacher, rather than tie things down.)

11. A period of silent reflection and a closing prayer, with an invitation to continue prayerful upholding of the preacher through the preparation process

The sermon preparation community is not a sermon-writing committee. The ultimate responsibility for sermon shaping resides with the preacher. The preacher is accountable to the community for careful listening, but not for issuing in the sermon a set of minutes or a joint resolution. At the beginning of future meetings, it will be helpful to ask briefly what group members heard in the sermon as preached, and how earlier hearings may have been reflected in that. (It will not be surprising if areas that surface in preparation for one sermon find their way into sermons preached later on.) Care is taken on the part of all participants to respect the confidentiality of the group. The preacher uses personal information only if explicit consent is given.

Some preachers or group participants might worry that a sermon following such discussion will be less interesting (like the second hearing of a story that was entertaining only the first time around). That is seldom so; the opposite is usually the case. Anticipatory energy is heightened—all have a shared investment in the sermon's unfolding. The sense of mutual support between preacher and participants is palpable. Even though such a process is not frequently practiced, I believe it is the ideal. Once having tried it, all may wonder why preaching would ever be undertaken any other way!

2. Active, Informed Listening During the Event

The middle stage of sermon listening is at once the easiest and the most difficult. It is the easiest because all that is required is focused openness from those already attuned to dynamics at work in the Spirit-ed conversation. It is the most difficult because, in a sound-bite culture, our senses are more barraged than engaged. Attention deficit disorder is as much a cultural phenomenon as an individual pathology. With all the noise to which we are continually subjected, it can be difficult to listen. We are manipulated by media, sometimes even consciously and willingly. We are also on guard against our own gullibility. We can be critically resistant and uncritically accepting at the same time.

There is no deep listening without critical listening. Genuine critical listening, however, has to do not with looking for something to criticize, but with knowing what to listen for, and how to interact with it. The first task of a listener is not to agree or disagree, praise or blame, but to describe in one's own terms what one has heard the preacher say. The primary question a listener asks is not, "What do I like or dislike?" but, "What am I hearing?" and then, "Where is this leading?" (Note how congruent this is with the requirements of stage 1 sermon play—soft focus preparation.) The next task is descriptive (rather than prescriptive) as well. The primary questions are: "How is the preacher making sense? What sermon-shaping strategies is the preacher employing that enable me to hear what I am hearing?" In short, "How does this sermon play?" More specifically:

- "What voices are represented in the sermon, and how do they converse with each other concerning matters of immediate and eternal significance?" This question looks at voices from several contexts:
- The Scriptures—the texts of the day in a context that makes them meaningful
- Cultural issues and icons—historical and current
- Congregational concerns—individual and corporate

- Other liturgical elements in the worship of the day
- The preacher's own experience
- "What literary/rhetorical instruments is the preacher using to orchestrate these voices?"
- Sensory images and metaphors
- Stories of human character in conflict
- Concepts and ideas set forth in reasonable arguments
- The sequence of movements through which images, stories, and ideas are plotted

A sermon hearer who engages those questions does deep critical sermon listening and participates in an unfolding Spirit-ed conversation of which the sermon, per se, is but a part. Such listening is both demanding and rewarding, a skill that develops over time, more in community than alone.

3. Discerning, Mutual Listening with the Preacher After the Event

A continuing discussion after the preacher has ceased speaking becomes the place where the sermon really begins! Participants now listen and speak concerning how all have heard God's Word, and how the sermon kindling has fueled subsequent hearings. God's Word comes to people through an extended conversational history that has been passed, torchlike, among members of communities in an extended trajectory of times and places. Sermons are a continuation of that dynamic dialogue. All hear God's Word better by talking back—and listening to nuances picked up by others.

This third stage of sermon listening is not, therefore, sermon evaluation, in the conventional sense. Every preacher can always improve in methods and techniques. The deepest need of preachers is for spiritual insight, much of which comes through conversation with members of the community who share in the preaching process. The best help a preacher can receive is not a critique of points, illustrations, ideas, or sermon strategies. Rather, as he or she hears listeners talk about what they have heard, the preacher, over time, develops sharper ears for listening during sermon preparation. Based on that deeper hearing, the preacher is able to speak God's truth more profoundly.

In such a discussion, the distinctive impressions of every group member must be honored. Consensus should not be pressed for (although it will often emerge if the reflections of participants are given space). Sometimes there will remain clearly divergent impressions and opinions. No matter. The Spirit can speak through respectful disagreement as well as through consensus. Trust in each other and in the process is required. Developing such trust takes time and patience. The following guidelines suggest a dynamic framing context within which such fire furthering can be effectively fostered:

1. Listen to the sermon carefully but do not take notes while it is being delivered. If convenient (especially if the discussion will not take place immediately), listeners can make a few notes afterward. The discussion will not be a test of who can remember the most. Latent recollections will be stimulated by the process of sharing observations in the group. (If a discussion group convenes at some time after the preaching of the sermon, the preacher can prime the discussion by re-presenting or recapitulating only the introductory paragraph.)

2. Select a listening/discussion facilitator. This may be someone other than the preacher, but it need not be. Since the sermon now belongs to the community, it is not inappropriate for the preacher to take the role of facilitator.

3. Begin (as in the pre-sermon discussion) with a few moments of shared silence.

4. Invite the preacher to cite immediate personal reflections about the sermon, and what kinds of observations would be specifically helpful. This initial response is brief, and does not include

145

elaboration, explanation, or justification of what has been said.

5. Share with each other descriptive recollections and impressions of the sermon. As in the pre-sermon discussion, it is important to limit responses to a single observation at a time from each person, especially at the start of the conversation.

6. Name ways the sermon sparked fresh awareness of what God's Word might mean, and where it might lead.

7. Talk about how the sermon was shaped and crafted, about what interpretive and rhetorical elements it contained.

8. Suggest ways the sermon might be fine-tuned or reshaped to foster an even clearer, deeper hearing of the Word of God that is already present or implicit.

The sermon discussion following these guidelines is focused, but freewheeling. It may well spark and stir up all sorts of insights that are beyond the bounds of the Scripture text or the sermon topic of the day. Difficult issues are not masked or skirted in interchanges shaped by a process such as this. Whether the issues are homiletical, hermeneutical, sociological, or theological, the discussion generates light, rather than heat. It takes practice for the process to become natural. When the process gets up to speed, however, it takes on a life of its own. When the moving energy embodied in the sequence of these steps is honored, the guidelines function as choreography for the dance of Spirit fire. As a practical matter (and for ensuring continuing energy in future discussions), it is best to set time limits on discussion periods. These guidelines are important for naming what a community can do to shape an upper-room space for inviting Pentecost fire. The way the process is presented to a sermon listening/discernment group and conducted in it, however, needs to be described more succinctly if it is to spark effectively.

In brief, the discussion proper moves through four stages, each generated by a particular question:

1. What are we still hearing?
2. Where might this be leading?
3. How does this sermon play?
4. Where might the sermon grow?

The first three stages are descriptive. The fourth includes a prescriptive, evaluative dimension, arising naturally out of the first three. These stages should not be presented as an evaluation form that folks fill out, turn in, and walk away from, leaving the preacher to make sense of and come to terms with! They are steps in a Spirit-ed conversation starter.

Responding to a Sermon

1. What are we still hearing? What do we continue to see, smell, taste, and touch—immediately and reflectively?

- Points
- Pictures
- Phrases
- Feelings
- Free associations
- Fresh insights
- Hanging questions
- High-energy spikes
- Centering chords

    2. Where might this be leading? Where, in God's name, are we going? Where does this seem to be taking us? What is the sermon's dynamic direction for us? What are we moved to do? For example, are we being led to perform one of the following actions?

- To offer thanks, praise, or petition
- To confess doubt, wound, or misdirected behavior
- To think further on, or differently about, an issue or issues
- To talk things over with others

- To plan, act, or enlist the action of others
- To agree, disagree, or press the issue

3. How does this sermon "play"? Through what strategies does the sermon help listeners make sense of the Gospel?

- As game—the play of Spirit-ed voices (An interaction of the Scriptures, culture, congregation, liturgy, and preacher)
- As music—the play of rhetorical instruments (An orchestration of images, stories, and arguments/ideas)
- As drama—the play of narrative plot (A sacred mystery of tension, sequence, and suspense)

4. How might this sermon grow? How can the good work begun in the sermon be even more effectively performed? What costs and benefits are involved in these patterns of sermon play? (There are no cost-free sermon strategies. What is gained or lost by those used?)

- Question posed to the preacher:
    - "How might this sermon look and sound when it grows up?"
    - "What changes in this sermon might produce the following results?"
    - A more vital center—a more energetic thrust
    - A more effective engaging of Spirit-ed voices
    - A more effective orchestration of rhetorical instruments
    - A more authentic plot—with respect to both the mystery of life and the mystery of grace
- Questions posed with the preacher:
    - "What seems distinctive in this preaching voice?"
    - "How does it seem to be developing over the time?"
    - "What possibilities and challenges might lie in store for this preacher?"
- Questions for continuing reflection:
    - "What other matters might we fruitfully consider?" (Issues exegetical, theological, social-political, congregational, pastoral, homiletical, communicational, personal)

148

———⇒➤●⬤◀———

Thus far, the space for tongues of fire that we have been shaping is more akin to the marketplace in Luke's Gospel than to the upper room. Luke's marketplace is the space for which the Gospel is ultimately intended. But because preachers are charged to go to such open spaces, it is also important that they participate in more intimate, upper-room spaces with other preachers. Preachers are not necessarily smarter or more spiritual than others. But those who share a common commission and frame of reference as kindling artists have distinctive experiences and insights. There are some things preachers can learn only from congregations; there are other things they learn more effectively through conversation with colleagues.

Yet not many preachers make good use of contacts with colleagues. Time and distance are factors (though e-mail makes the latter less of an excuse). But preachers are often shy about sharing their work with one another ("I don't mind standing before my congregation, but I get nervous if I have to preach in front of colleagues"). If they do critique each other, they tend to resort to generic compliments, or vague, abstract suggestions. Or to say, "Do it this way—just like I do." Who has the time for that? But if there are common kindling points for distinctive fire building such as we have been describing, then preaching colleagues can provide significant spiritual and professional support to one another.

We can serve each other as Eli and Elizabeth. You remember Eli. As he comes to the end of his life, he has been less than successful as parent and as priest. Yet when Samuel comes to him in the middle of the night, saying, "Here I am! You called me," Eli senses whose voice he cannot hear, and has the grace to send Samuel back, with hints for listening in the right direction. And something else as well: Eli has the perception and courage to charge Samuel, "Come back and tell me what you hear—regardless of the possible consequences" (which are considerable) (1 Sam 3:1–18).

Then there is Elizabeth. You remember the most unusual day her young relative Mary had, once upon a time. When the angel Gabriel comes to Mary with unsettling news, it is all Mary can do to blurt out (being "much perplexed" at the angelic greeting): "How can these things be?" and "Let it be with me according to your word!" The angel, before taking leave, makes a further announcement—one, I suspect, with a suggestion implicitly tucked in: Elizabeth is living with God's unsettling word as well. Mary departs "in haste," heading for the home of Elizabeth. Elizabeth meets and greets her—and, knowing what is taking place within herself, names what is taking place within Mary. Mary, inarticulate until this point, promptly bursts forth in the Magnificat (drawing resources, in the process, as Luke tells the story, from her preaching great-great-grandmother Hannah).

The functions served by Eli and Elizabeth are not gender specific. Eli helps Samuel pay attention to what he does not clearly recognize or understand. Elizabeth confirms for Mary the Word whose Source she clearly has discerned, but understandably is reticent to share. All of us who preach are in continuing, healthy need of both types of support from preaching colleagues. What a grace to offer or receive such midwifery! How do these kindling transactions take place? By creating spaces of intentional nurture. Once again, therefore, here are some guidelines suggesting points of departure.

Serving as an Eli or an Elizabeth
Listening Preaching Colleagues into Living Sermon Words

1. The listener invites the preacher to describe how the sermon is unfolding in his or her understanding. The listener shapes a space in which the preacher can fruitfully explore the tension, trajectory, and centering energy of the sermon.

2. The listener asks evocative questions concerning the play of the

emerging sermon:

- The voices it engages (the Scriptures, culture, congregation, preacher, liturgy, and so on)
- The senses it integrates (image, story, and idea/argument)
- The plot it unfolds (the sequence of action scenes and the suspense of grace discovery)

3. The listener raises questions regarding what he or she is not clear about, and responds to questions the preacher has about the sermon.

4. The listener poses questions the sermon raises for him or her—which is not the same thing as making objections. (In a well-established, trusting relationship, points of disagreement can perhaps be named. Dealing with them is at the preacher's discretion.)

5. The listener may offer suggestions to illuminate places where the preacher feels stuck. The listener may not, however, radically redirect the focus of the sermon unless that is invited by the preacher.

Eli does not tell Samuel either what Samuel has heard, or what the revelation means. He helps Samuel recognize and attend to God's word to Samuel, regardless of the consequences that word may have for Eli. Elizabeth names what is happening within Mary, after which Mary breaks forth in the Magnificat.

———————⇒⊱⊰⇐———————

The outbreak of Spirit fire comes as and when it wills. There are no techniques at our disposal for guaranteeing its appearance. What we can do is to create conditions conducive to the fire's kindling, and to sustain burning once the fire has descended. (That, I think, is what the disciples were about in the upper room.) The question remains, "Is Spirit-ed conversation, where sparks go off in all directions, what

151

Luke intends in his depiction of Pentecost?" I have filled in the blanks of the story, but I had an active imagination as an adolescent; perhaps I still have not grown up!

Yet I think a plausible case can be made, from Luke's own writing, for seeing the preaching of Pentecost as something other than solo performances by disciples and passive spectator responses from their audiences. After all, Pentecost was not a one-day, point-in-time event. The doctrine of the Holy Spirit is not a point at all, but (like Moses's burning bush and pillar of fire) a dynamic process, that can only be tracked as an energizing, illuminating trajectory. That is what Luke gives us in the Book of the Acts of the Apostles; and the trajectory of the Spirit's fireworks he sets forth says something to me about how those fireworks got off the ground in the first place. I have three events in mind, way stations in the evolution of the Spirit's work in the shaping of the church: Philip's conversation with the Ethiopian eunuch in Acts, chapter 8; Peter's surprising encounter with the Roman centurion in chapter 10; and the convening of the Jerusalem Council in chapter 15.

Philip is in the midst of a successful preaching mission in Samaria. People are listening "with one accord." Those who have been paralyzed by factors natural and supernatural are being released and remade. There is "great joy in that city." Suddenly the Spirit pulls Philip from his fire tending, and sends him into the wilderness. (Can the Spirit really know what the Spirit is doing? This does not look like good stewardship of preaching energy!) In the middle of nowhere, Philip happens upon a man who seems to have everything, economically and politically, but is, in fact, twice marginalized. He is not a descendant of Abraham's, and he cannot procreate descendants of his own. Yet he has come a great distance to participate in the worship of God's covenant people. Did he make it to Jerusalem and get caught up in the fireworks display? If so, was he left on its fringes as well?

Whatever this man's Jerusalem experience, it is clear he has

152

continued to take the initiative. He has procured a scroll of Isaiah's prophecies. Reading them aloud as he journeys home, he hears the prophet somehow speaking to his condition. Well, now the Spirit's mysterious movement is clear! Philip has been called away from a successful preaching mission to undertake a highly strategic evangelistic move! Philip joins the eunuch's chariot, sits alongside the man, and preaches a conversational sermon, one-on-one. That sermon turns out to be not just more successful, but more conversational than Philip could have imagined! Listen to Luke: "As they were going along the road, they came to some water; and the eunuch said, 'Look, here is water! What is to prevent me from being baptized?'"(Acts 8:36).

No less a Lukan authority than Fred Craddock fills in some of Luke's open space. "What prevents you from being baptized?" In one of his sermons, Craddock has Philip answer thus within himself: "Everything! You are a foreigner, not a covenant player. I have no authority from headquarters to initiate you as a full-fledged member of the fellowship of the Messiah!" But then, Craddock suggests, Philip realizes that the eunuch has only connected the dots—provided, in his own words, the inescapable conclusion of Philip's sermon. So there is nothing Philip can do—confronted with the implications of his preaching that the eunuch makes explicit—but to draw a deep breath and say, "Nothing prevents you from being baptized—nothing at all!" The eunuch speaks back to Philip's sermon, and Pentecostal fire flames up as the Spirit intends.

The names and faces are different in Acts, chapter 10, but the pattern is analogous. Peter, hungry and awaiting lunch, falls into a trance; has a disturbing, thrice-repeated vision; and is commanded by God to treat as clean what he has heretofore understood to be unclean. The meaning of the vision becomes clear with a knock on the door by an emissary of a Roman military commander: a commission to take the Gospel to another foreigner—one at a greater distance

153

from the covenant than the eunuch. Off Peter goes, sermon in hand, only to find that God has gotten to Caesarea ahead of him. Cornelius speaks back to Peter before Peter has a chance to get his sermon out. So Peter tears up the manuscript and starts over, preaching one directed primarily toward his own further conversion: "I truly understand that God shows no partiality, but in every nation anyone who fears him and does what is right is acceptable to him" (Acts 10). (Have you ever set out to preach to your people, and ended up, with their gracious help, discovering that the message was more for you than for them?)

It all comes together at the convening of the Jerusalem Council. There is "no small dissention and debate," Luke says in Acts 15, about the complex, momentous question of covenant identity. Folks with competing points of view weigh in. After Barnabas and Paul have borne witness to how God's Spirit has come not just to, but through, various Gentile believers, James, the community's leader, issues his edict: "Listen to me!" But this is no authoritarian edict! James gives voice to prophets long since departed. He acknowledges the legitimate concerns of the theological-social conservatives. He also names the creative, playful new work of the Spirit—expressed by new believers indirectly through the advocating voices of Barnabas and Paul. When the verdict is rendered—"Therefore I have reached the decision that we should not trouble the Gentiles who are turning to God" (along with the culture-sensitive corollaries of that decision)—what James says turns out to be the sense of the meeting. Everyone involved has been speaking back and doing serious listening as well.

None of those Pentecostal preachers—Philip, Peter, Barnabas, Paul, or James—is a lone ranger, a solo performer. The preaching that takes place in all these places is clearly Spirit-ed conversation—a continuing dialogical dynamic of listening and speaking in which meaning emerges through ongoing interaction. And, for that reason,

I think it not irresponsible to suggest that the character of the Pentecostal kindling event itself was much the same—and normative for Christian preaching.

Most of us have been brought up to respect what is, at one level, a reasonable and practical convention of social intercourse: "Don't everybody talk at once! We talk with each other by taking turns. First you will speak, and I will listen; then I will speak, and you will listen." It is, after all, very hard to hear anyone if everyone is talking. But that sensible convention masks a deeper truth: "If you are talking, you aren't listening; and if you are listening, you aren't talking" needs to be complemented by its apparent opposite, "Unless you are 'talking' you aren't listening; and unless you are 'listening' you aren't talking." Whatever could that mean?

If you are speaking with me, I cannot really hear you unless, in my head, I am doing a kind of simultaneous translation—recasting your words in an interpretive frame of reference that honors both where you are coming from, and where I find myself. Similarly, if I have any hope of communicating with you, I must, even as I speak, be listening to how I am articulating, and to how you seem to be receiving. To take place at all, communication by conversation has to be communal.

Preaching, at its best, is not filling space with a speaker's words, but shaping space, through a speaker's words, for listeners to fill in as the Spirit prompts. Sermons are kindling points for sacred fire play.

9

Angel-Touched Offerings, Coal-Touched Lips

The angel of God said to [Gideon], "Take the meat and the unleavened cakes, and put them on this rock, and pour out the broth." And he did so. Then the angel of the Lord reached out the tip of the staff that was in his hand, and touched the meat and the unleavened cakes; and fire sprang up from the rock and consumed the meat and the unleavened cakes; and the angel of the Lord vanished from his sight. Then Gideon perceived that it was the angel of the Lord. (Judges 6:20–22)

In the year that King Uzziah died, I saw the Lord sitting on a throne, high and lofty; and the hem of his robe filled the temple. Seraphs were in attendance above him; each had six wings: with two they covered their faces, and with two they covered their feet, and with two they flew. And one called to another and said:

*"Holy, holy, holy is the Lord of hosts;
The whole earth is full of his glory."*

The pivots on the threshold shook at the voices of those who called, and the house filled with smoke. And I said: "Woe is me! I am lost, for I am a man of unclean lips, and I live among a people of unclean lips; yet my eyes have seen the King, the Lord of hosts!"

Then one of the seraphs flew to me, holding a live coal that had been taken from the altar with a pair of tongs. The seraph touched my mouth with it and said: "Now that this has touched your lips, your guilt has departed and your sin is blotted out." Then I heard the voice of the Lord saying, "Whom shall I send, and who will go for us?" And I said, "Here am I; send me!" (Isaiah 6:1–8)

156

For all our talk of Spirit fire, we have spent most of our time devising strategies for sermon play. More on text attending, plot shaping, wordsmithing, and discussion convening than on opening ourselves to the presence of God. Sermons and sermon discussion don't transform lives, God does—and by grace, not by human sermon work (no matter how playful). God works through limited, broken speech; and God often brings the rhetorical powers of preachers and the professional prowess of homileticians to naught as well. We began this adventure in metaphorical preaching methodology with a sweeping vision of creation fire, and of what transpires when the consuming / not-consuming fire of transcendent presence touches finite creation. As we shifted focus to the process of sermon preparation, I pledged we would return to the creative, adventuring, communal, liberating vantage point that is not a conceptual, propositional, or rhetorical point, but a pulsing energy point. All the techniques we devise for shaping a Spirit-ed conversation are but means to build an altar in preparation for the descent of fire. Preaching is about participating in a power beyond our understanding and control. On the one hand, there are no dodges from the task of individual sermon preparation and long-term professional skill building. To say, "We are only vessels. Any positive impact of preaching is solely by means of the Spirit," though pious sounding, is not particularly Spirit honoring. But to speak of preaching as mystery is not a perfunctory religious-jargon nod in the direction of what is really no more than human scholarly and artistic expertise and insight.

Yet if to speak of the mystery in preaching is neither simply a convenient way of abdicating our responsibility for a discipline, nor a way of asserting our mastery of it, then what do we mean by mystery when it comes to preaching? We could address that question through a systematic conceptual analysis of divine human interaction. That would not be inappropriate, for this issue is at the heart of any theology affirming a God who transcends creation and yet is immanently involved with it as well. But rather than engaging the question abstractly, let's walk alongside two colleagues with experience of the mystery toward which we wish to gesture.

Gideon is in hiding, covertly threshing grain so that it won't be seized by the marauding military forces of Midian. Gideon's vision and intentions are limited (and not irrational under the circumstances): he'd like to keep from being killed, and he'd like to keep on eating. Threshing grain in a winepress is strategic to both. An angel of the Lord interrupts the proceedings with one of those unsettling greetings: "Hail, mighty warrior! The Lord is with you!" "With respect, wrong on both counts!" is Gideon's grim reply. "I am weak, and the Lord does not seem to be around. Midian's might is evidence for my assessment, not yours!" (Judg 6:11–24).

The angel responds as though Gideon's reproach has not even registered: "Go with all your strength and rescue Israel. I am sending you myself." "But how?" asks Gideon, trying again. "My clan is the weakest in my tribe (which itself is none too strong), and in that clan, I am the least important." "You can do it because I am with you," comes the response (with no explanation concerning what "with you" might mean). "If the Almighty One is with you, the force of opposing thousands is of no more significance than a single soldier. Look again, Gideon, the odds are in your favor."

There seems little point in arguing; but Gideon tries the best he can. "Show me some proof!" Gideon gamely insists. "Don't go off and leave me till I come back with a food offering for you." "Agreed!" the angel says; and off trundles Gideon to put together a little something on the spur of the moment. Gideon does well, all things considered; generously, also, given low resources and high threat levels. He presents what he can put before the presence of the Lord. The angel tells him where to put it, touches it with his staff, and the offering turns to fire. The angel disappears, and Gideon begins to realize what he has encountered. So begins one more episode in the long line of God's creative, communal, liberating adventures with those God refuses to cease loving. Gideon is weak; he offers what he has. His offering is not just incinerated; it is taken and transformed.

Isaiah's story is somewhat different from Gideon's (no two stories are alike). When accosted by God's presence, Isaiah is not in hiding, but in public; not working, but worshiping. Times are not as bad for him; he has no reason for fear. Yet when his epiphany comes, his terror level far trumps that of Gideon's. The awesome power of "the Lord, high and lifted up," together with the piercing "Sanctus!" cries of circling seraphim—it all but freezes his blood. Gideon's response to God is, "I am weak!" Isaiah's is, "I am unworthy!" God's moves in these encounters are different as well. To Gideon directly, God simply declares, "You will go!" In Isaiah's hearing, God asks, "Who will go?" and waits until Isaiah responds: "Here am I! Send me!" How God's fire plays with each differs also. Gideon's offering is turned to flame (and he begins to realize that God can work with weakness). Isaiah's lips are touched with fire (and he begins to realize that God can work with unworthiness as well).

I am taken by yet another difference in these two call narratives. Though both of those called identify in some respects with their communities, Gideon's identification is primarily by comparison. He starts with an assessment of the community, and ranks himself against it: "We are all weak here, but I am lower in the political pecking order than practically anybody else." Isaiah's identification is more radical. He begins with himself ("I am a man of unclean lips"), then moves toward the community in solidarity with it ("I dwell among a people of unclean lips").

The point of these comparisons is not to evaluate, but to describe. I find both call and fire stories illuminating in my own preaching life because each speaks to what I have come upon (or what has come upon me) time and again, in ways that are always and never the same. What I seek to gesture toward is an experiential mystery named in two complementary ways by another preaching colleague whose name is Paul:

• We know that all things work together for good for those who love God, who are called according to God's purpose.
• God's grace is sufficient for me, for God's strength is made perfect in weakness.

Both reflections apply to circumstances in which I find that I lack competence or credibility (as Gideon confessed), and to situations in which I am aware of my lack of moral or spiritual virtue (as Isaiah recognized). It is precisely Gideon's sense of weakness that God exploits in subsequently directed strategies for defeating the Midianites ("Your army is far too large, Gideon! Send most of them home. That way there will be no question as to where the strength for victory has ultimately come from!"). It is exactly Isaiah's sense of unworthiness (and his identity with community) that gives him what he needs, empowered by God's coal of fire, to craft and communicate prophetic words that can cleanse but do not incinerate (when, apart from a sense of sinfulness, it would be easy to light the latter rather than the former).

In experience analogical to Gideon's, I have discovered that one way my limited preaching skills have been touched and transformed is through recognition that no one is fully adept at playing with fire. The torches of the community are needed for adequate illumination and power. That in itself is a healthily humbling transformation of whatever offerings I manage to prepare. I have to bring the offering, prepared as best I can, open to the understanding that, touched and set alight, it will become something more than it was before, something to which I have contributed, but that is not my own. Analogously with Isaiah, I find that whenever I get in regular rhythm, serving as faithfully as I can in the house of my God, something happens in the broad context of my living as a preacher that makes me overwhelmingly aware, not only of my weakness, but also of my unworthiness. And that recognition works its way into a reshaping of my vision and a recasting of my words, requiring and enabling me to preach as one who is within, among, with, and for my fellow listeners, rather than to or at them.

In the call narratives of Gideon and Isaiah—stories gesturing toward the mystery of divine-human interaction—prophetic leaders undertake the work that God has invited them to after they recognize who they are and how they stand before God. There is no question as to whether their best efforts are involved, but no question either about where the ultimate energy comes from. Gideon and Isaiah tend and transmit the fire; they don't create it.

Paul's declarations regarding the mystery of divine-human interactions (particularly insofar as they involve proclaiming the Gospel) explicitly suggest what is implicit in the Gideon and Isaiah stories: that the transformations for good in which strength is perfected in weakness occur within preachers in the very act of their sermon preparation. It is not just that human efforts are touched with additional assistance, and sent on their way successfully. The connection is more intimate. Something is forged and refined in us as we forge and refine our sermons. We become different, and through that difference, God does something we could not have done all by ourselves.

What, in that, is what we do, and what God does? The answer differs, surely, from preacher to preacher, and from sermon to sermon. Sometimes, retrospectively or even in process, we can point to particular elements in the interactive dynamic. Sometimes we are too close (or God has been too close) for us to have much perspective on who is responsible for what. What is clear is that God honors what we do (as with Gideon), and asks us for our participation (as with Isaiah). And that God has a hand in our sermon writing, working together for good; but that, however skilled our efforts and seasoned our sensitivities, they are constantly being perfected by a fire beyond our power to kindle.

Although this sounds mysterious, it is not without human analogue. If you have ever collaborated with a colleague in a project—no, better, if you have ever really played with a group of playmates—you know that something larger than anyone involved lifts the enterprise into a larger life. If you have ever played, you have an intuitive, visceral, by no means irrational understanding of what these words are gesturing toward.

And that may be one reason why regular interaction with preaching colleagues—both congregation members and other professionals—is essential. Not just as a means of signal checking and skill building (though those are important). Not just as a means of fellowship, morale, and mutual encouragement (though those are essential also). But primarily as a tangible reminder of the mysterious power that continually touches what we do and transforms it, and as an ongoing witness that in preaching, we are always playing before a Presence that we do not control.

Though we do not control what God does in and through us and our preaching, we can, over time and in professional conversations with colleagues, track some of the movements in our preaching lives, and through that tracking make ourselves available to the Presence, who comes to us in epiphanies of retrospective discernment. Keeping a focused homiletical journal can be a good way of having kindling materials ready to hand for ignition from falling sparks.

The Homiletical Journal:
"Sketchbook" for Preaching Imagination

Keep a weekly record of ongoing reflections—informal, but focused with respect to various dimensions of the preaching life. Set aside a specific writing time and space each week. Address two areas each week, and shift the focus, as appropriate, over time. Include items such as these:

- First impressions of the lessons for next Sunday (sparks for preaching)
- Homiletical observations on a sermon heard during the week
- Images, events, insights, and experiences of potential homiletical significance (from newspapers, magazines, TV shows, conversations, chance observations and encounters, and so on)
- Issues, ideas, and observations arising out of readings for, or participation in formal courses of study
- Personal struggles, successes, frustrations, and visions related to your particular vocation as a preacher

Use whatever form suits your purposes: a computer, a notebook, a sketchbook, or note cards, for instance. Feel free to draw diagrams or pictures, or to write in incomplete sentences and phrases, so long as what you produce will be intelligible upon rereading. It is unnecessary to bring entries to closure, though you may find that putting things down in fact focuses impressions and ideas that have been playing peekaboo at the fringes of consciousness.

Lightly scan your journal segments from time to time, to stay in touch with places you have been. You might give passages a closer look (either analytical or meditative) when you go on a professional or personal retreat. It often helps to page through entries when you are feeling uninspired with respect to a particular sermon.

Although a journal is not a filing system for sermon illustration, you may be surprised at how specific materials will pull on you when they are relevant. The lived context in which they were recorded will probably be as efficient for search purposes as more abstract categories (or even more efficient than such categories).

The highest value of keeping such a journal is as a means of tracking the trajectory of your journey as a preacher—which is simply another way of saying how God has led you and been present to you in your role as a chosen fire sharer.

163

10

Making All Things New

*The one who was seated on the throne said, "See, I am making all things new." (*Revelation 21:5)

Freedom, community, adventure, and creativity. A delight in the fiery dance of elements integral to play does not have to be carefully taught. Indeed, as the song from *South Pacific* tells us, it is hate and fear that have to be taught. Destructive forms of play are perpetual, but not natural. Play is cross-cultural, apolitical. It is not even unique to humans; all creation bears witness to its playful Maker's heart. Time and again, as *imago dei—homo ludens*, we are "surprised by joy" (as C. S. Lewis says), gifted with experiences that bring both deeply satisfying peace and inconsolable longing. We glimpse the glory of God's playful fire through significant interchanges at work, in informal conversation with friends and family, sometimes even in worship services that turn out to be less boring than expected. Every once in a while, joy strikes us suddenly, like spontaneous combustion. With our inherent need to play, we also schedule periods of recreation (an important discipline, surely). Yet, however delightful vacations may be, sooner or later it is back to work, a return to the grind, nursing fond (selective) memories of what it was like when we used to engage in child's play.

The longing for a space to play can produce a predictable drudgery of its own—prepackaged recreation programs designed to ensure that we take a break, get away from it all. Often those become occasions of anxiety. So much of who we long to be as *homo ludens* is projected on the scheduled play times we call vacations ("Are we having fun yet?")! That preoccupation further intensifies a longing for what (as Lewis notes) seems always to recede just beyond the horizon. (See *Surprised by Joy: The Shape of My Early Life*, by C. S. Lewis, New York: Harcourt, Brace, and World, 1955.)

In their efforts to make the world a safe place for playing, nations and peoples get caught up in coercive counterfeits of play that take on a terrifying life of their own—fires out of control in a radically different sense than the one described in chapter 9. Caught in the grip of such deadly play, the whole creation, St. Paul tells us, groans in travail—"waits with eager longing for the revealing of the children of God." War games can generate an instant rush that feels like play. But things look different from the other side of the contradictory creativity of which war is the ultimate transfixing signal.

Military forces were still beating up on Baghdad as I wrote this chapter. A "Quote for the Day" that I downloaded from the Internet edition of the *New York Times* provided, early in the conflagration, a revealing reality check on that play from the vantage point of an officer: "It's a little sobering," the captain confessed. "You're in training for this, you joke, you can't wait for the real thing. Then when you see it, when you see the real thing, you never want to see it again." Therein lies one of war's greater cruelties—the eventual epiphany of what a hoax it is. If *imago dei* is *homo ludens*, then, in warfare, play is cancerlike—life turned in on itself. The Scriptures call such deviance sin.

What, then, of the war and the destructive fires as set forth in the Scriptures? Devastating fires, ultimately imputed to God, are found there in abundance. From warnings of immanent doom descending on the wicked (for example, in Amos, chapter 1), to visions of all existence as we know it annihilated (for example, in 2 Peter, chapter 3), to bits of both in apocalyptic images of hell (for ex-

165

ample, in Revelation, chapter 20).

Perhaps what Luke records of the urge to incinerate shown by James and John finds its way occasionally into the perspectives of various biblical authors. (None of God's prophets, after all, are put forth as free from partisan misperception or misuse of sacred fire—Elijah comes again to mind.) It is also likely that God's prophets gesture toward a reality more powerful than any force that physical or human nature can produce, arguing, metaphorically, not literally, from lesser to greater. (It is instructive, in this regard, to note that by the time we get to Amos, chapter 7, the prophet is entreating God to spare the land from fire—an intercessory request that God agrees to grant.)

This, at least, is clear: Avenging and avaricious fires are ultimately self-destructive. What we sow, we reap; what we ignite, as human beings, we cannot contain as selectively as we would like. The fires of God's judgment that biblical artists paint may be understood as setting forth, on cosmic canvas, a vision of where misplaced play with fire inevitably leads—toward the eventual self-immolation of every unjust advantage ever taken. That is a solemn warning when we are tempted to take destructive advantage over others; it is a comforting assurance if we are tempted to despair when we are burned by destructive advantages that others take. When play becomes a means of domination, it eventually undermines everyone involved.

It is well to remember that St. Paul counsels the same treatment for enemies that Elisha prescribed for the armies who sought his life. Protected as he was by chariots of fire, you remember, rather than annihilate his enemies, Elisha ordered that they be given food and drink and then released. Was Paul recalling that when he enjoined, "If your enemies are hungry, feed them; if they are thirsty, give them something to drink; for in so doing, you will heap burning coals upon their heads" (Rom 12:20). Is that vengeance? Perhaps it is a participation in God's relentlessly redemptive "vengeance"—a fighting of sinful fire with purifying holy fire.

A dear colleague of mine lost his wife to a protracted battle with cancer. They had both agreed that on her death, she would be cremated. At first the image was impossible for him. Then he was able to envision cells of cancer being consumed, and his beloved released, refined, and remade as she ascended into larger life.

The ultimate Christian hope is the promise of re-creation. When counterfeits of healthy fire play seem all-consuming, that hope can sound far-fetched. Good stories begin, "Once upon a time," and conclude, "And they all lived happily ever after." When we are surrounded by battle lines and protracted suicidal conflict, "They all lived happily ever after" can sound like escapist fantasy at best. It is well to acknowledge, once again, that playing with fire is a dangerous metaphor for preachers. Yet it is one from which we cannot shrink. As T. S. Eliot puts it succinctly:

> *The only hope, or else despair*
> *Lies in the choice of pyre or pyre—*
> *To be redeemed from fire by fire*
>
> *We can only live, only suspire*
> *Consumed by fire or by fire.*
> (from "Little Gidding")

"Behold, I am making all things new!" says the One who is the light of the holy city coming down from God—the same sole and sufficient source of energy that brought the world to birth. But notice how the re-creation process is undertaken, as the author of Revelation depicts it. New heavens, new earth, the new Jerusalem descend from God—not by a single, instantaneous wave of a mighty magic wand, but by the tender, patient act of wiping tears from all faces—a task much more intimate and time-consuming. In other words, "They all lived happily ever after" is not simplistically true for the story of creation

167

any more than it is simplistically true for any story we have actually lived (or found interesting to listen to).

Of the four evangelists, the Johannine author is the one most concerned with assuring his listeners of the happily ever after. Jesus is in charge throughout. He has (and doesn't hesitate to offer) all the right sermon answers (often answers to questions his listeners aren't asking—but would ask, if they knew what was good for them!). So I am fascinated by his treatment of one extended episode. What might we learn by listening to it?

> *A certain man was ill, Lazarus of Bethany, the village of Mary and her sister Martha. Mary was the one who anointed the Lord with perfume and wiped his feet with her hair; her brother Lazarus was ill. So the sisters sent a message to Jesus, "Lord, he whom you love is ill."* (John 11:1–3)

We need read no more; we know how the story goes from scene to scene, and how it turns out in the end. In some versions of the Bible, the story goes by the title "The Raising of Lazarus." At first hearing, the Lazarus episode sounds like a perfectly straightforward case of happily ever after. (Lazarus does, after all, come back from the dead. How much better can it get?) But the longer and closer we listen to how the story unfolds, the stranger this Evangelist's sermon becomes. Before long, in fact, it doesn't sound much like happily ever after at all.

Consider the opening, situation-setting, character-designating sentence: "A certain man was ill, Lazarus of Bethany, the village of Mary and her sister Martha." So far, so good—it does what good stories, and good sermon plots, are supposed to do: set a context, quickly, cleanly, deftly. But notice what comes next: "Mary was the one who anointed the Lord with perfume and wiped his feet with her hair."

Maybe this is just the preacher's way of reminding us of who Mary is and what she has been up to. (That kind of reminding is an

168

established technique in the repertoire of storytellers and sermon shapers: jostling listener memory in a complicated pattern of unfolding events.) So let's turn back in the text to see where he has introduced Mary previously. Back we page—chapters 10 through 7. Nothing. Let's start from the beginning—nothing in chapters 1 through 3. Was it in the middle? A check of chapters 4 through 6 turns up empty as well. Where is Mary? She's in this sermon somewhere! Paging ahead, we find that the events alluded to at the start of chapter 11—Mary's anointing of Jesus—do not even take place until chapter 12! Is this odd, or what? John the Evangelist has stolen his own thunder—gotten ahead of himself, given us a later scene (the anointing sequence) before he even gets this scene (the resurrection sequence) off the ground. Either this preacher needs to retake Homiletics 101, or something strange is going on. That's not the way sermon plots are supposed to unfold! But this is only one homiletical oddity in an exceedingly curious sermon.

In the opening scene of the sermon plot, Lazarus is sick, and Jesus deliberately delays coming. Well, that seems strategically defensible—it is part of a good plot structure; it piques the listener's curiosity, heightens suspense. Yet such a delay seems out of sync, not only with the dynamics of emergency medicine, but also with the character of Jesus. He has a reputation for being the great physician, not a doctor who dallies. The sermon crafter does have Jesus say that the delay is "for God's glory." But that sounds rather as though Jesus is jerking Mary and Martha (to say nothing of Lazarus) around, using their desperate situation to make a theological point. Jesus looks bad—so does the fourth Evangelist. Good preachers don't manipulate story lines for moralistic purposes, or push their characters into being preachy.

When he gets to Lazarus's tomb, Jesus weeps. Not just once, twice, or even three times does the sermon author bring this to our attention; we hear it four times over. This surely means that when we get to the supposedly triumphant punch line, uttered at the door of the tomb—"Lazarus, come forth"—we are intended to envision the stains of Jesus's tears still etched in the sweat of his face. If that is so, then when Jesus raises Lazarus, the sound we will hear is not the "Hallelujah Chorus," but the wrenching sob of utter anguish. Yet in this preacher's treatment of him, Jesus is almost always in total control (even before Pilate and upon the cross).

But notice who says nothing: Lazarus. Step out of the sermon for a brief side glance: in a cemetery near Washington, D.C., there is a life-sized sculpture of Lazarus emerging from the tomb. No delight or excitement lights up his face, no jaunty "I'm baaack!" His expression is a mixture of dazed disorientation and stark terror. Perhaps we have filled in the Evangelist's sermon space with a happily-ever-after pose that isn't there! Might the sermon writer be opening a different kind of space? Might Lazarus's reaction be a suggestion that, unless there is more to resurrection than coming back to live happily ever after, it isn't worth the cost for anyone involved? Just because one is cured of a mortal illness (even after mortality itself), it doesn't follow that one has been deeply healed. Just because you're breathing, that doesn't mean you're living. Whatever the Lazarus story is in the hands of this Evangelist, it isn't a happily-ever-after.

Now let's go back to the misplaced Mary piece of this striking story—both go back, and look ahead. It is almost as if the Evangelist is so intent about the deepest meaning in his sermon that he just can't wait to telegraph it early (regardless of what his homiletics professor happens to think). Maybe this preacher wants listeners to be clear that what they are hearing is not happily ever after in any straightforward sense.

Lazarus is raised, the sermon shows us (and leaves it right there, with no further explanation or application). Then, as the sermon continues, folks gather for a meal. Lazarus is there. (Both he and the preacher remain silent regarding how Lazarus feels about returning

to life after being dead.) This is not a happy meal. Death is in the air—
it is so thick, in fact, that the stench of its certainty is all but suffo-
cating. Jesus is a marked man. His raising of Lazarus has pushed matters over the edge. Everyone anticipates what is coming, much like
the world hangs horrified just before the onset of inevitable war.
What, after all, do you say at supper with a dead man talking? Jesus,
as good as condemned already, is having the equivalent of a last meal
with these friends.

Into this impossible scene, where she has no place, comes Mary,
proceeding to behave in a way that does not fit. She anoints Jesus's
feet. Mary is not looking to escape the threat of death. Surrounded
by the stench of death, she is celebrating, here and now, the fresh
smell of eternal life. How? Why? Perhaps because, to the preacher of
this sermon, she has heard, in her grieving over her lost Lazarus,
words of Jesus's that intimate an altogether different take on happily
ever after: "I am resurrection—I am life. Those who believe in me,
even though they die, will live, and everyone who lives and believes
in me will never die" (Jn 11:25–6).

Does the preacher intend us to understand that Mary fully
grasps what she hears—either when she first hears it, or when she
anoints Jesus in anticipation of his own impending death? Not likely.
I think that, through his portrayal of Mary's experience, the fourth
Evangelist invites us to envision a new mode of being, one in which
"even at the grave we make our song," as we say in our burial rites. Not
a triumphant, fire-invoking war song. But a fire-of-love song that en-
ables us to distinguish, and to participate in, a process of being re-
deemed from fire by fire.

"Behold, I am making all things new!" That is what creation's
God announces at the conclusion of an account of re-creating history that, from Genesis to Revelation, leads from fire through fire to
fire. The difficulty with the happily-ever-after version of that story
(the one so vulnerable to being tragically misconstrued) is that it is

too abstract. When those triumphant words are uttered—"Behold, I am making all things new!"—they are intended by the preacher (and by the preacher's God, I think) far more radically, and far more literally, than most of us can bear or dare to take them. Happily ever after, as nostalgia for, or justification for defending the way things used to be in the good old days is not just wishful thinking, it is dangerous thinking. "Every idea of [God] we form, [God] must in mercy shatter," C. S. Lewis tells us (C. S. Lewis, *Letters to Malcolm, Chiefly on Prayer*, New York: Harcourt, Brace and World, 1963, page 82).

"All things new" is a difficult vision toward which to preach. Our words must gesture from burned-out places toward an unfolding trajectory we can only see "through a glass darkly." And yet our preaching is not simply a report of God's creative and re-creative actions from the past, a naming of those actions in the present, or an announcement of God's promises for the future (although it does involve all of those). Preaching points toward fire, but through playing with fire, it also participates in God's creative kindling work.

Time and again, I have found this true in my preaching life, but never more palpably so than on the Sunday afternoon I was asked to preach at a parish near the Pentagon less than two weeks after the terrorist attacks of September 11, 2001. The lives of many in the immediate area, including parishioners, were devastated. The church had been holding several services daily. After ten days, however, the clergy felt that the time had come for a "service of closure." I was invited to offer the sermon at a celebration of the Eucharist using lessons appointed for the burial of the dead. It was important to shape in the service a hospitable space for mourners of all religious traditions, and of none.

The sermon kindled on that occasion gestures toward what, I believe, is central in the vision and work of those who are who called to play with fire.

Mourning for Victims of September Eleventh
Isaiah 61:1–6, Psalm 27, Revelation 21:1–7, Matthew 5:1–16

"Oh, my God! What are we going to do now?" That is the question we instinctively ask when all of a sudden our world blows apart. "Oh, my God! What are we going to do now?"

The first time we ask the question—as fireballs flare, and towers collapse—the answer is spontaneous, thoughtless, wordless. Our bodies do the talking—hearts pound, faces freeze, muscles jerk. We do not pause to consider the options; the answer is automatic: "What are we going to do now? Duck and run—get out of here!"

But there is more to this question than a first response can give. The question comes again, a second time: "What are we going to do now?" And maybe because it's our job, what we get paid to do, but more likely because it springs from an instinct as deep as self-protection, a second answer comes to the second asking: "What are we going to do now? Reach out and help!"

There's not much calculation in this response either. "It'll look great on my résumé." "My mother will be so proud." "Tough job, but good pay." No—none of the above. Rather, the raw imperative of pure human freedom: "They're in danger; I gotta go. I must do something—whatever I can—whatever it takes!"

But the question doesn't go away with answer number two. Indeed, the very answer offered in heroic rescue action rekindles the question with greater force: "Limited success, dwindling hope, lives lost, loves torn. What are we going to do now?"

And another answer makes its way into our asking space, still spontaneous, but now more measured: "Mourn and weep." And so we have done, since that unforgettable Tuesday—wells of tears brimming in our eyes, floods of tears falling from our eyes, eyes of all ages, all races, all religions (and no religion). Eyes of women, eyes of men (unashamed tears from males, for a change). Tears of grandfathers,

173

aunts, children, neighbors—tears of citizens from many nations. Every tear appropriate—no tear wasted.

Has anyone ever told you, "That's nothing to cry over!" "There, there—don't cry," or, "You stop that crying, right this minute!"? Well, maybe someone has at some time or another. But I'll bet no one has said such things to you in the last few days. "Oh, my God! What are we going to do now?" "Mourn and weep."

"Mourn and weep"—but once again, the answer regenerates the question. So many people mourning and weeping—"What are we going to do now?" As the question goes deeper, a deeper answer comes as well. "Hug and hold." Stricken though you are, you can embrace the stricken. You don't have to flash a "no scars" badge. Your own scars credential you for hugging and holding the wounded and weeping.

But after that—then what? "What are we going to do now?" A cascade of options spills across the mental screen: "Storm and rage!" "Strike back!" "Hunker down!" "Put it behind us and just get on." So many options, none without reason, not all contradictory—but not all compatible. And this may be why we have witnessed and shared still another dimension of "going and doing" in recent days: stopping what we're doing and sitting still. Not the sitting still of paralyzed fear, dazed stupor, or sheer denial, but a stopping and sitting to honor and treasure rich resources no violent attack can ever destroy—good deeds done, lives of grace lived—unrepentant lanterns, shining in a dark world.

But stopping and sitting still has meant something else for us, I think: a deliberate determination to pause and reflect, before moving on. Do you hear it coming—the question again, "What are we going to do now?" This is a time to sit and be still, so that the question can work its way down to who we deeply are, and who we wish to become.

We are told we need closure, so that we can begin to put our lives back together and move forward. In some ways, surely, we do need closure. But there are significant respects in which closure on "the recent tragic events" (as they are already being tagged) is as in-

174

appropriate as it is impossible. Even if a return to business as usual were an available option—which, of course, it is not—few of us would want to go there. Too much has been de-centered, too much is up for grabs, too much is at stake. "What are we going to do now?"

But how can we explore the abyss of that question, if all we have to listen to are the sounds of our own voices, reverberating in the echo chambers of our own minds? If all we have to draw on are words pouring forth from the media—shrill, strident words demanding our hearing? Perhaps there are other voices who might be invited to join us in the questioning journey. Voices of those pushed beyond the breaking point of senseless suffering, inflicted by violence, terrorism, cruelty. Voices of those we call people of faith. Voices that might not tell us just what we wanted to hear. But voices that might help us hear what we need to do.

"Speak to us, elder sisters and brothers! We have not been, most of us, in a place like this before. Speak to us—we have need of your company—need of your wisdom."

And listening, as we have today, to the voices of a songwriter, a poet-prophet, a subversive teacher, and a wide-eyed visionary, here are things we do not hear: an executive order—"Now Hear This!" (to which the answer can only be, "Yes, sir; whatever you say, sir!"). This is also what we do not hear: empty, pious platitudes—"Just trust God; it's gonna be all right." No—what we hear are strange words, words quiet and wild.

"The Lord is my light and my salvation, whom then shall I fear? One thing I seek—to dwell in the house of the Lord all the days of my life." Not an escape from chaos, a cozy cave in which to ride out the storm, but "the house of the Lord"—a dwelling place, a living space, an energy center for a journey through hell. "Show me your way, O Lord," the songwriter sings. "Because I do have enemies; Oh, God, lead me on a level path."

Where will that level path lead us? Another voice, the voice of a poet-prophet, offers an answer: The level path will lead us "to bring good news to the oppressed. To bind up the brokenhearted. To proclaim liberty to captives"—not only to prison inmates, but also to long-time victims of economic and political oppression. God's "level path" will lead us, the poet-prophet suggests, to counter works of terror with a curious vengeance—the proclamation of God's radical peace. To comfort mourners, to rebuild ruined cities—not just to rebuild towers from rubble, but to dig through, as Isaiah says, the devastation of many generations, the devastation that fires acts of terrorism and violence.

Hold it! Time out! Wait a minute! We are in no position to do that! "Indeed you are," cuts in the voice of the subversive teacher. "Blessed are the poor in spirit, those who mourn. Blessed are the meek (those who don't have arrogant answers at the tips of their tongues). Blessed are those who want righteous justice (fair distribution, not quick retribution)—blessed are those who want righteousness so badly they can all but taste it. Those who long for justice so deeply they feel pangs like those of a stomach that hasn't eaten for days, like a dehydrated body, desperate for water.

"Blessed are those who show mercy—regardless. Blessed are those who work for peace—whatever it costs." "Blessed" *not* in the sense recently used by the president's press secretary when he said, "The citizens of our country have a blessed life" (which is not, anymore, true in quite the way it was when he said it!); but "Blessed are we." You and I are in the best possible place, the most strategic position to realize that the Reign of God is a commonwealth more real than anything else around.

And then, if that's not overload enough, here comes the word that is really wild, prefaced by a sight too good not to be true. A new heaven and a new earth—free from horror and carnage, a new city coming down from God, coming down to connect with the reaching-up work of mourners, mercy messengers, peacemakers. A new city, proving, once and for all, that heaven has nothing to do with "pie in the sky bye and bye."

But wait—that isn't all. The word comes again: See—the home of God is among mortals. See—God dwells among human beings, God will be with them, as they belong to God. And—oh, look—do you see that? God wiping every tear, one by one, from every weeping human eye! Let's take a deep breath, so we can take this in: Wiping tears—not saying, "Stop that crying!" But wiping tears from eyes blinded by pain, and grief, and rage. Wiping and wiping—tear after tear—for as long as it takes, for as many who weep; so that all can turn with fresh eyes, and behold God's new city.

"Behold—I am making all things new!" That's what God says, as God wipes away tears. That is a closure worth having! And that is the only closure with a chance in the world, because it is a closure that opens toward utterly new life.

Impractical? It all depends how you define the word. Frankly, in these voices, I hear a clear sense of direction. A marching order I can salute—freely and gladly—with all that I am and all that I do.

What I am hearing is this: When our fingers touch the tears of inconsolable suffering, then our fingers are in touch with the finger of God. And if the only way our fingers find to dry the tears of some, is to do what makes others weep—well, it is just possible that what we will hear is a firm, quiet voice saying: "See here! I am busy drying tears! It is not necessary to bring tears in order to dry tears. On this one—either you are with me or you are not."

"Oh, my God! What are we going to do now?"

"Oh, dear God! Please help us do what we need to do now!"